MULTIPLYING
GENEROSITY

Creatively using insurance
to increase legacy gifts

Marlena McCarthy
with Jack Bergmans

civil sector press

Library and Archives Canada Cataloguing in Publication

McCarthy, Marlena, 1959-, author

Multiplying Generosity: Creatively using insurance to increase legacy gifts / Marlena McCarthy with Jack Bergmans.

ISBN 978-1-927375-30-3 (paperback)

1. Fund raising--Canada. 2. Life insurance--Canada. 3. Charities--Canada--Finance. I. Bergmans, Jack, 1960-, author II. Title.

HV41.9.C3M33 2015   361.7068'1   C2015-907189-5

Multiplying Generosity: Creatively using insurance to increase legacy gifts

Published by Civil Sector Press, A division of The Hilborn Group
Box 86, Station C, Toronto, Ontario, M6J 3M7 Canada
416.345.9403 www.charityinfo.ca

Editors: Lisa MacDonald with Janet Gadeski
Cover Art: John VanDuzer
Interior Design: Cranberryink

To Jeanne-Mance and Len McCarthy,
loving parents who taught me the importance of
living my dreams, and giving generously

Acknowledgements

There are several people critical to the creation of this book.

First and foremost, thanks go to our partner Judy Doré, the inspiration for creating Bequest Insurance. In 2011, Judy (an experienced financial advisor and insurance broker) asked us why people don't utilize the power of insurance more often to create super-sized legacy gifts. This simple question led us all down a path that answered this question, unearthed several problems, and then revealed many solutions that are crystallized in this book.

Great appreciation goes to Paul Nazareth whose constant encouragement led the Bequest Insurance team to understand how important our work really is in opening up more effective ways of helping people to be as generous as they can by using insurance in creative ways. We also thank Paul for his critical feedback on our manuscript.

Our sincere thanks also go to Judy Doré, Malcolm Burrows, Frances Buczko, and Aneil Gokhale for thoughtful reflections on the manuscript which helped to make the book better.

Special appreciation goes to Sandra Mimic, who shared her thoughts about the manuscript and her own inspirational story of giving a powerful gift of life insurance to her alma mater.

We are grateful to the Canadian Association of Gift Planners for bringing together fundraisers and professional advisors alike in the shared goal of helping people fulfill their philanthropic dreams. The Bequest Insurance team appreciates being embraced by Greater Toronto CAGP members, who generously welcomed us to CAGP and shared their thoughts, challenges, and successes of giving through insurance. Their input and workshops inspired Jack and I to dig deeper into the topic.

Finally, thanks go to Jim Hilborn of Civil Sector Press for realizing that the world needs a book that clearly explains the complex practice of marrying insurance with philanthropy, and for helping us to get this book into the right hands. Our gratitude also goes to Lisa MacDonald, Kathleen McBride and John VanDuzer for helping to shape, polish and give birth to the book.

Table of contents

INTRODUCTION

Anyone serious about leaving a significant gift to charity should consider using insurance.

A Bequest Insurance client, Frank, approached us in 2014 about making a legacy gift to a small charity he has led and volunteered with for decades.

At age 71, Frank was examining his finances, knowing that he'd have to convert his $42,000 registered retirement savings plan (RRSP) into a registered retirement income fund (RRIF), from which he must withdraw a percentage every year as taxable income. He and his wife know they didn't need this income to cover present nor future expenses, or provide for their children. They decided to use the annual RRIF income as charitable gifts and if there were any remaining funds, they would gift any residue to the charity in his Will.

Bequest Insurance's financial advisors talked to Frank about his options. If he followed through with his plan, his mandatory RRIF withdrawals (an average of $3,360 a year) would whittle all this money away in twelve and a half years, leaving nothing left to give as a bequest.

Frank asked what would happen if he cashed out his entire RRIF to make a one-time charitable gift. His advisor warned him that this money would all become taxable income, push him into a higher tax bracket, and increase his OAS pension claw back to $6,553 that year. Also, after Frank paid the tax on his RRIF income, he'd only have $29,400 left to donate. Frank quickly dismissed this idea.

Bequest Insurance's financial advisors offered Frank a creative solution that would allow him to leverage his registered savings into a much larger legacy gift for his charity – *and cost him nothing to do so.* Here's what we did.

We helped Frank make use of an insurance strategy called a "back-to-back" (or insured annuity). First, we helped Frank to purchase an insurance policy that requires premiums to be paid until Frank dies, because it would offer the greatest gift to his charity. To ensure his pre-authorized premium payments are always covered, we moved his $42,000 RRIF into a registered annuity. It generates $3,360 in annual income for life, which is automatically deposited into the same account from which Frank's pre-authorized premium payments are taken.

Frank's annuity income pays for a life insurance policy that is immediately worth $53,000 – an amount that will start to grow after a few years. Frank assigned his charity as the policy's owner and beneficiary, earning him a charitable tax receipt for the $3,360 he pays each year in premium payments. His tax credits eliminate the income tax Frank must pay on his RRIF's annuity income, and also reduces a small amount of income tax on his other income, leaving him with an improved net income each year!

In summary, here's the real beauty of using insurance to give a charitable donation:

Frank turns $42,000 in registered savings into a legacy gift of at least $53,000. After a few years, the value of his policy is likely to grow by a few thousand dollars every year. If Frank lives to 100, his charity could receive at least double the amount of his original investment, and possibly much more. Because this type of donation is outside Frank's estate, it won't be diminished by probate-related fees or taxes.

Frank's policy is guaranteed never to lapse because his annuity income is directly deposited into the chequing account from which his premium payments are automatically withdrawn.

The death benefit from Frank's insurance policy will go to his charity within two to three weeks of the insurance company receiving the insurance claim.

In the end, Frank will be able to offer his charity so much more because he made his gift using insurance, instead of turning his mandatory RRIF deductions into annual donations, and assigning any residue to his charity in his Will.

Here is another way to look at what Frank's outcome could be:

Comparing possible outcomes	Frank donates annual RRIF income to charity	Frank buys an annuity and donates a life insurance policy
Frank's annual income	$98,912	$98,912
Annual taxes	($23,021)	($23,021)
OAS clawback	($4,098)	($4,098)
Charitable tax receipt	$3,360/yr for 12.5 yrs	$3,360/yr for life
Net income	$71,793	$71,793
Charity receives	$29,400	$53,000 to $100,000+

So why aren't more people using insurance to leave powerful legacy gifts?

Earn
CONTINUING
EDUCATION
Credits

Take the companion online course to earn CE credits.

Details here: https://tinyurl.com/ce-credit-course

FOREWORD

I'm a professional fundraising writer and a member of the Canadian Association of Gift Planners and the Association of Fundraising Professionals. One of my specialties is the promotion of different planned giving tools – and in particular, gifts of insurance.

I'm married to Jack Bergmans, a Canadian Certified Financial Planner and member of the Canadian Association of Gift Planners who is an expert in integrating philanthropy into his clients' financial and estate plans, and using insurance to its best advantage to meet and whenever possible exceed their goals.

Jack and I co-founded Bequest Insurance with Judy Doré, an experienced financial advisor and insurance professional who is also a member of the Canadian Association of Gift Planners. Together, we have become experts in giving through insurance.

Jack and I felt compelled to write this book because there is no other book in North America that explores this topic in depth, and translates "insurance-ese" into everyday language. We think it is needed. Our conversations with countless fundraisers and financial planners have taught us that many don't really understand how beneficial it can be to integrate insurance products into financial and gift planning, or how to use insurance to its greatest advantage.

Many fundraisers are also worried that they will be gifted with policies that will simply fail if donors stop paying their premiums.

Many gift planners admit, "I find giving through insurance complicated. Apart from mentioning to donors that they can donate a paid-up policy, I'd prefer not to talk about this, since I'm nervous about being asked questions I can't answer."

Others have told us, "Most of my donors only want to give gifts through their Will. Why shouldn't I help them do what they want to do?"

This book will answer all of these questions and concerns.

Giving using insurance is the second most popular way for Canadians to make estate gifts. Yes, this only constitutes about 5% of planned gifts, but if more people understood the benefits of giving in this way, and got advice that allowed them to structure effective and guaranteed gifts, charities could get larger gifts leveraged by insurance.

Donors can take advantage of benefits that can far outweigh giving through a standard bequest. I'll just tantalize you by saying donors can often use insurance to give bigger gifts than they could have imagined, which go quickly to their charity after their death. These gifts aren't diminished by taxes and probate-related fees, and donors receive generous tax breaks (either during their life or to benefit their estate) that allow them to leave more to their heirs. And that's just scratching the surface of the benefits using insurance in charitable giving.

This book will guide you through all the ins and outs of giving through insurance, how to identify donors that can benefit from using insurance as a philanthropic tool, how to easily talk to them about this beneficial option, and how to administer insurance gifts.

I'll also be very transparent about some of the risks involved in accepting some gifts of insurance. You'll learn how you can counter possible pitfalls, and get information and tools you can use to minimize or eliminate risks.

One challenge you may face is that many financial advisors working with your donors — even those who specialize in insurance — don't really understand the many ways to use insurance products to help their clients meet their financial and philanthropic goals. In fact, *many financial advisors don't even ask their clients about their philanthropic goals because they feel it's either "too personal" or "too technical."*

Our companion volume, *Ripple Effect: Growing your business with insurance and philanthropy*, is an educational tool you can lend or give to your most trusted financial advisors. Jack Bergmans has written this comprehensive guide for financial advisors to teach them how to form deep and enduring relationships with their clients by helping them experience the profound happiness that comes from supporting charitable causes they truly believe in. And by providing holistic advice that meets all of their clients' goals, advisors will also gain more business through referrals.

Although the insurance and tax laws Jack mentions are Canadian, the overall concept of integrating insurance into financial and estate planning is common to any financial planner in any country.

So if you want to ensure the financial professionals on your charity's committees, boards and preferred lists are fully up to speed on gifts of insurance, you stand to benefit by giving them a copy of this book.

Simply put, whether you are a gift planning newbie or old pro, this book will help you deepen your conversations with donors...revealing options that may remove obstacles donors have to giving, and opening the door to meaningful gifts that have an outstanding impact.

Marlena McCarthy

What fundraisers will learn from this book

Written in easy-to-understand, conversational English that you can use in discussions with your donors, you'll gain a firm grasp on everything you ever needed to know about giving through insurance, annuities, and other insurance products.

1. **Incredible benefits of giving through all insurance products.** So enticing that you'll even consider making your own estate gifts in this way.

2. **The pros and cons of establishing a life insurance program in your charity.** Decide whether proactively promoting gifts of insurance is good for your charity.

3. **Insurance 101:** An easy-to-understand primer on insurance.

4. **Using insurance for charitable giving:** The most common ways to use insurance to give more, leave more to other beneficiaries, and disinherit the taxman.

5. **Creative uses for insurance to enhance charitable giving.** Details the back-to-back strategy, and many other options that offer donors great benefits.

6. **Types of people best suited towards giving through insurance.** It's not for everyone. Learn for whom it's suitable to bring it up.

7. **Promote gifts of insurance better.** Help your donors learn the benefits of giving through insurance, and if it can work for them. Donor talking points will allow you to confidently speak to donors and answer common questions.

8. **Effectively administering your insurance giving program.** Step-by-step guide to accepting and effectively handling gifts of insurance, and stewarding these donors.

Chapter 1

THE BENEFITS OF GIVING
THROUGH INSURANCE

"It is one of the beautiful compensations of this
life that no one can sincerely try to help another
without helping himself."

— Charles Dudley Warner, American writer

Tell me why I should promote gifts of insurance.

Insurance is a powerful financial tool. When combined with legacy planning, it offers both donors and charities incredible benefits that can't often be achieved by making a traditional bequest.

The "Bequest vs. Insurance Gift" face-off

The traditional bequest

One of your donors, a healthy 68-year-old woman, shares with you that she is leaving your charity the proceeds of a Guaranteed Investment Certificate (GIC) through a bequest in her Will. She bought the GIC at her bank. It is currently worth $35,000 and is making 1.5% interest. When she dies, this GIC will have appreciated in price somewhat.

> (i) *Not understanding some of the financial or insurance terminology? We've included a Glossary for your review.*

This may sound good to you. However, before your charity gets this bequest, your donor's executor or tax advisor must initiate the probate process, which places a value on the donor's final estate, and requires the appropriate probate taxes and related fees (legal and/or accounting) to be paid. Then on your donor's final income tax return, taxes must be remitted on this GIC and all her other assets. After all this, the bequest shrinks to much less than $35,000. Depending on how long it takes for the executor to complete all of this paperwork, you'll probably get the donor's bequest a year or more after your donor's death – and maybe up to four years from residents of the Canadian province of Ontario (*see Appendix 2*).

Leveraging the same gift using insurance – *Everyone wins, except the taxman*

If your donor makes use of a simple insurance strategy, she can use her $35,000 to leave a $50,000 legacy gift, which won't be lessened by taxes, probate taxes and related fees, or lawyers' or accountants' expenses, and will be delivered to your charity in less than a month.

In this scenario, your donor transfers her $35,000 GIC into a savings account with an insurance company and assigns your charity as the beneficiary of any residue remaining in the account when she dies. She then buys a $50,000[1] life insurance policy, naming your charity as its owner and beneficiary, and arranges to have the premiums automatically deducted from her savings account.

These funds will completely pay off her policy in 10 years. Even if your donor dies before the policy is fully funded and therefore self-sustaining, your charity still receives the full death benefit of $50,000[2]. And, if there is money left in the savings account when she dies, you'll get that too. When your donor passes away, your charity will receive this legacy gift within two to three weeks of an insurance claim being filed on the policy. Typically, this donation cannot be contested by anyone other than a dependent spouse or child.

Better yet, because the proceeds of her policy are a charitable donation, your charity's tax receipt will provide her estate with $25,000[3] in tax credits. This tax savings allows the donor to leave more to her beneficiaries, which could include other charities.

---

1 The value of any life insurance policy depends upon an individual's age, health, and if he or she smokes. This example is based on a healthy 68-year-old female non-smoker buying a policy in 2014.

2 Exceptions: Within two years of getting a life insurance policy, if the insured takes his or her own life or dies of a medical cause not revealed to the insurance company before their insurance policy was issued, usually the beneficiary only receives the amount the insured has paid into premiums.

3 Tax credits from charitable donations vary according to the province or country in which donors live. This example uses a 50% tax credit rate.

Talking to your donors about the benefits of using insurance as a donation

Whether a donor lists your charity as the beneficiary of a life insurance policy, an annuity, variable annuity, cash savings or any funds (e.g. GICs and segregated funds) invested in insurance company, the benefits are the same.

To make it easier to talk to your donors about this topic, I've written about the benefits of using insurance as a donation in language you can use with your donor.

1. **You get to do good, on a big scale.**
    By purchasing a life insurance policy and making a charity the recipient of the policy's death benefit, you can turn affordable (and possibly tax-deductible) monthly premiums into a very large gift, *for a fraction of what you've paid in premiums.* You'll be remembered for making a significant impact on the work of your charity.

2. **Attractive tax benefits.**
    If you assign your charity as the owner and beneficiary of a life insurance policy, all your premiums are tax deductible. Your charity will issue tax-deductible charitable receipts for 100% of the value of your premiums, reducing your taxes every year.

    If you assign your charity as the beneficiary (not owner) of your policy, your estate will receive a tax receipt for the entire death benefit. In this case, your premiums are not tax deductible. However, your estate will benefit from a large tax deduction that will reduce your final year's taxes. Or if the tax credits are greater than those taxes owing, your executor can use the extra credits to get a refund on taxes paid in the year before your death. This will allow you to leave even more to your heirs.

If you have funds in any other kind of insurance product, you can name your charity to be the beneficiary of any funds remaining when you pass away, which will generate charitable tax credits that will lower your estate taxes and allow you to leave more to your heirs.

3. **Purchasing insurance products is free.**
By using an independent and unbiased insurance broker who understands how to incorporate philanthropy into estate plans, you'll get free sound financial advice that is personalized to your circumstances, and offering the best price or rate of return currently available in Canada. You won't be charged any fees to set up insurance policies or investment accounts – your advisor will be compensated by the insurance company for the work he or she does for you.

4. **You don't have to change your Will to make a charitable gift of life insurance.**
Assigning your charity as the beneficiary, or owner and beneficiary of any insurance product doesn't need to be mentioned in your Will. However, since your executor does have to supply a death certificate to your insurance company to ensure your donation is released to your charity, it is wise to leave your executor instructions on any insurance policies or accounts that you have. It can be wise to leave insurance policy or account information for your executor with your Will. (Note: for an example of such instructions, see *Appendix 3.*)

5. **Your insurance gifts occur outside of your estate, and go to your charity quickly and easily.**
Upon your passing, your generosity benefits your charity usually within two to three weeks* of the insurance company receiving a copy of your death certificate.

In contrast, cash bequests left in the Will are significantly decreased by probate-related fees and taxes, and creditor claims, and may take from nine months to many years to get to your charity.

Note for charities with Ontario-based donors: As of January 1, 2013, changes made to the Ontario Estate Administration Tax Act (normally referred to as "Probate") allow the Minister of Revenue to *assess or reassess an estate for its tax payable for four years after the application for probate is made (see Appendix 2).* Since your executor is responsible for the distribution of your assets, he or she may want to wait for four years to ensure that there are no emerging challenges to your estate assets. In that case, your bequest may not get to your charity for four or more years. This makes a compelling case to arrange to have your donation made directly and quickly through an insurance product.

6. **An insurance gift is private, usually incontestable and creditor-protected.**
   Because this gift doesn't occur through your Will and goes directly to the named charitable owner or beneficiary, creditors and heirs cannot challenge your donation or make claims on these funds – with the exception of a spouse or child whose illness makes him or her wholly dependent on you for their survival.

   If giving anonymously is important to you, gifts of insurance are ideal. While you are alive, only your charity and your executor need to know of your generosity. And if you wish to be publicly acknowledged after your passing, you can arrange this in advance with your charity.

7. **Your insurance gift is not diminished by probate tax or related legal and accounting fees.**
   Your insurance donation will be larger than gifts that flow through the Will and donor's estate.

8. **When donating a life insurance policy, your gift is guaranteed.**
Canada's life insurance companies are as highly regulated as our banks. You can be assured that your charity will usually get your insurance gift within two to three weeks of your executor informing your insurance company of your death.

9. **Gifts of insurance can offer huge benefits to younger donors.**
You don't need to wait until you're older and accumulated significant assets to make a large gift with the leveraging power of insurance. Younger and healthier donors can buy more insurance for less money, and take advantage of smaller (and possibly tax-deductible) monthly payments.

10. **You can easily change your mind.**
If circumstances change and you want to change the beneficiary of your gift of insurance, it's easy, free and fast to complete a beneficiary change form with your insurance company. In contrast, to change a bequest left in your Will, you must hire a lawyer.

11. **Assigning your charity to be the residual beneficiary of your annuity is a win-win.**
Like many people who are 50 and older, you may begin to worry about having enough money to last you the rest of your life. Purchasing an annuity, which gives you guaranteed payments for the rest of your life, can be a solution to your worries. And by making your charity the beneficiary of whatever remains in the annuity when you pass away, you may also be able to do good, and generate a tax credit that can reduce your estate taxes.

Benefits to your charity of promoting gifts of insurance

Here are seven excellent reasons why it's unwise to exclusively promote legacy giving through traditional bequests.

The bequest-related problems noted below can be reduced if donors use guaranteed life insurance and insurance products to make their gift outside of their estate.

1. A bequest written into a Will is not a guarantee that your charity will get it.

   - **Donors can lose interest in your charity** as their priorities change in life, leading them to name another charity.

   - **They can become annoyed with your charity.** Perceived poor customer service or stewardship, lack of information on how their donations are used, or an organizational faux-pas that gains negative media coverage can all lead donors to change their Wills. Or your donors may be shocked to discover that all your charity's workers are not all unpaid volunteers and that some staff make a salary that they feel is much too high.

   - **Dwindling funds may cause donors to eliminate bequests** using their assets to cover living expenses or to leave more to loved ones. But if a donor has already fully funded a life insurance policy and has named your charity as its owner and beneficiary, you will be guaranteed to receive the policy's full death benefit when the donor dies.

   - **There are a surprising number of donors' kids expecting that the entirety of their parents' residual assets will pass on to them.** It is always unexpected, but fundraisers have told me stories that in a bequest donor's final days, children have gone as far as convincing their confused mother that her charitable bequests are inappropriately large or simply unnecessary, and show up at Mom's deathbed with a lawyer and a revised Will to sign. This sounds horrifying, but it happens more often than you'd care to imagine.

Yes, it's true that a donor can easily change the beneficiary of a gift of insurance. But if they make your charity the owner (or irrevocable beneficiary) of their insurance gift, you're guaranteed to get the gift within two to three weeks of the executor making a claim with the insurance company.

2. Charitable beneficiaries of Will proceeds can be contested.

The prospect of getting an inheritance can make people do out-of-character things. Beneficiaries can dedicate themselves to finding a loophole surrounding their benefactor's bequests, or claim that their benefactor was not in his or her right mind when signing their Will. Or, if a charitable beneficiary is not clearly named (e.g. "The Cancer Association") a tug-of-war can ensue between charities with similar names. Contested bequests can be tied up in messy legal proceedings for years.

Typically the only person who can challenge a gift of insurance is a dependent spouse or child.

3. Lawyer's fees, executor's costs, creditors, probate taxes and federal taxes can eat away at traditional bequests.

In comparison, the final value of an insurance gift is guaranteed and normally will not be diminished by taxes, fees, or creditors' payments.

4. Bequests from Ontario donors may be delayed by four or more years.

Changes to the Ontario Estate Administration Tax Act allow the Minister of Revenue to assess or reassess an estate for its tax payable for up to four years following the executor filing for probate.

Gifts of insurance do not fall under this amendment. (For more information, see *Appendix 2*.)

5. Giving through insurance may allow your donors to leave your organization significantly larger gifts.

    Life insurance can have a multiplying power that allows a relatively small investment to provide a huge tax-free death benefit that can grow even larger over the donor's lifetime. In addition, because insurance benefits are guaranteed to be paid out to the policy's beneficiary, your charity will still receive the full value of the policy's death benefit. The only exceptions are explained in *Chapter 3*.

6. If your charity is in dire straits and is the owner and beneficiary of a gifted policy, you can surrender the policy and use its cash value for current needs.

    The same cannot be done with a charitable bequest made through a Will.

7. If your charity is the owner of a gifted policy and the donor stops making the payments, it is possible that if the policy has accumulated sufficient cash value, these funds can be used to convert the existing policy into a fully-funded policy for a lower death benefit. This will likely provide your charity with a larger gift than simply collapsing the policy and claiming its cash value. Depending on the circumstances surrounding the policy, your charities may seek other donors to take over the premium payments. For more information, see *Chapter 4*.

In summary, introducing the idea of using insurance for charitable giving to your donors can result in a win-win situation:

*   Donors will be happy to leverage their donations into much larger, guaranteed gifts that go swiftly to fund your good works.

- Your charity will be able to do more with these guaranteed gifts, especially those that are dramatically increased by taking advantage of the multiplying power of insurance.

Chapter 2

THINGS TO CONSIDER
BEFORE ESTABLISHING AN INSURANCE GIVING PROGRAM IN YOUR CHARITY

"To give away money is an easy matter
in any man's power.
But to decide to whom to give it,
and how large and when,
and for what purpose and how, is neither in every
man's power nor an easy matter."

— Aristotle

Is actively promoting gifts of insurance right for my charity?

The benefits of giving through insurance are compelling. But before you recommend to your Board that your charity plunges headfirst into heavily promoting giving in this way, consider these points.

Distinct advantages of an insurance giving program:

- **Donors get it:** Donors generally understand life insurance. Most will already have insurance policies, so you don't usually have to explain the concept to them from scratch. In addition, if they like the concept, they will engage in a more detailed discussion about this with their financial advisor, so you don't have to know everything about insurance to promote gifts of insurance.

- **Multiplying power of insurance:** If someone uses life insurance as a way of leaving a bequest, the value of the policy may grow exponentially over the donor's lifetime. This can result in a final gift that is many times larger than the amount paid in premiums, making this way of giving a win-win for both donor and charity.

- **Psychologically appealing:** Because a gift of insurance is often paid in increments and the final value can grow over time, these gifts can be very appealing to donors who want to be considered a major donor but can only make modest gifts during their lifetime. In *Chapter 6*, you'll learn more about other types of donors who would find giving in this way very attractive.

- **Emergency cash:** If your charity runs up against dire financial circumstances and requires an immediate cash infusion to survive, donated life insurance policies owned by your charity can be cashed out, even while the insured policy donor is alive. Alternately, if you only need a portion of the cash value, you can take out what you need and still get the face value of the policy upon the donor's death, minus the cash that was deducted.

- **Get it fast:** Your charity may get gifts of insurance in a fraction of the time it takes to receive a bequest. You'll get the gift within two to three weeks of an insurance claim being filed on the policy. Between probate and possible challenges to bequests by other heirs, getting a traditional bequest can take four years or more.

- **Hard to challenge:** With few exceptions, it is impossible for donors' heirs to challenge or change a gift made through any type of insurance product, since the ownership or the beneficiary designation on the gift is irrevocable after the donor's death. Insurance gifts also have possible creditor protection ensuring debt collectors don't get to your gift before you do.

- **Easy administration:** Administering gifts of life insurance are relatively easy for a charity to administer. I'll go through this in detail in *Chapter 8.*

- **Unexpected early gifts:** This may sound morbid, but not every insurance donor will live to a ripe old age. Any actuary will assure you that the law of averages will mean some gifts of insurance will come to fruition earlier than you may expect.

- **Value guaranteed:** If a life insurance donor dies prematurely, your charity still usually receives the full value of their policy. There are some exceptions that I'll explain in *Chapter 3.*

- **Not considered fundraised income in disbursement quota:** In Canada, the Canadian Revenue Agency (CRA) does not consider death benefits you receive from gifted policies or residue from insurance products to be fundraised income when your charity is calculating your disbursement quota. The Canada Federal Government's Income Tax Act also specifies that the value of an unmatured life insurance policy (that is not an annuity contract) is nil, for the purposes of the 3.5% disbursement quota rule. Reference: CRA's Tax Bulletin No. IT-244R3 (#6-8) – "Gifts by Individuals of Life Insurance Policies as Charitable Donation" and Government of Canada's Income Tax Regulation #3702 (1) (vi).

Possible challenges in running an insurance giving program

- **Will annual funds suffer if donors divert monthly cash to paying insurance premiums on a gifted policy?** There is no proof that this will occur. In fact, donors that Bequest Insurance has helped to make an insurance gift care so much about their charity that they still make annual gifts. In *Chapter 4*, you'll learn about many ways that people can use life insurance and other insurance products to make charitable gifts that have no impact at all on annual giving.

- **Longer wait for the planned gift:** If a donor wants to purchase a policy specifically for the purpose of charitable giving, they usually must be under the age of 80. They must also be *relatively healthy* – they cannot have a significantly debilitating or terminal illness. This means that the typical donor who qualifies for life insurance will be younger than many of your other bequest expectancies, so the donation could be many more years in coming. In *Chapter 7*, I'll guide you through how to manage a program that can result in gifts that may come decades into the future.

- **Inflation may take a bite:** If an insurance gift takes decades to come to fruition, the guaranteed death benefit of an insurance gift may be diminished by inflation. However, if a donor is using life insurance that grows over time, then this growth may well outpace inflation.

- **Lapsed policies:** If a donor's financial or personal circumstances change, or they develop a negative opinion of your charity, they may stop paying premiums on a gifted insurance policy, and the policy may lapse and its value could be diminished or lost. Your organization can handle this situation in different ways, and should think this through before accepting certain insurance policies as gifts. In *Chapter 8*, I'll help you develop organizational policies to effectively deal with insurance gifts.

- **Not all insurance agents will give donors the best advice:** In the case of many failed policies, donors were advised to purchase pay-for-life policies because advisors unfamiliar with using insurance for philanthropic purposes apply the same rules to insurance purchases used for other reasons: buy the largest policy the client can afford, with the lowest monthly premium. Without a strategy in place to ensure the premiums on donated policies can be paid, the policy may lapse and become worthless.

  These agents don't understand that for a typical person buying a policy for a charitable purpose, paying their premiums feels like a donation. Many don't know that most donors do not donate to the same charity on a regular basis for their entire life – donors' priorities, interests, and personal and financial circumstances change over the years. The companion book to this one, *Ripple Effect: Growing your business with insurance and philanthropy* could make an excellent gift for your favourite advisors, helping them to understand donor psychology, and more effectively integrate insurance into their financial strategies with their clients.

- **Knowledgeable staff:** Are your charity's gift planning officers knowledgeable enough about giving using insurance to properly identify the donors who can most benefit from giving through insurance? Thankfully, this guide can bring both inexperienced and experienced gift planners up to speed on the best use of gifts of insurance.

- **Low interest rates lead to more expensive insurance policies:** During periods of low interest rates, purchasing insurance is more expensive. However, even in times of low insurance rates, there continues to be keen interest with donors who like the idea of using insurance to leverage a bigger gift for their charity.

- **Dogged devotion to one insurance company or agent:** Donors or charities may favour one insurance company over another, but when it comes down to getting the best product for the best price (since both change regularly) it is better to use an insurance broker to shop the entire market. Many charities keep a list of insurance agents or brokers who understand how to effectively incorporate insurance into estate planning and charitable giving, should their donors ask for a recommendation.

- **Your charity knows that you have been made the owner and beneficiary of a policy, but you may not know when the donor has died:** Like any other kind of bequest expectancies, it is important to keep in touch with insurance donors, and ensure that paperwork explaining their insurance gifts is located with their Will, so they will get in the hands of their executors. *Appendix 3* supplies you with a sample document that can be personalized by a donor to inform his or her executor of a gift of insurance.

- **Not every donor qualifies to give gifts of life insurance:** People who are 80 and up, and those with certain illnesses typically cannot get life insurance. However, people of any age, who are insurable or not, can easily assign their charity to be the beneficiary of any insurance products they already have. Read more about how to identify people who are best suited to give through insurance in *Chapter 6*.

Chapter 3

INSURANCE 101

"Fun is like life insurance.
The older you get, the more it costs."

— Kin Hubbard, American cartoonist

I need to learn more about insurance to talk to donors intelligently about it.

Almost everyone has a basic understanding of insurance. In fact, almost everyone has at least one kind. You may have insurance on your home, apartment contents or car, a life insurance policy, mortgage or credit card insurance to cover debts in the case of premature death, or group health, critical illness or disability insurance through your employer.

Later in life, many people buy annuities, an insurance product that guarantees income for life.

Other people invest their money in insurance company products like savings accounts, guaranteed investment certificates (usually known as GICs) and segregated funds (the insurance industry's version of mutual funds). Many Canadians trust insurance companies with their investments because they are as highly regulated by the government as our banks. In fact, investing money in insurance products can offer more advantages than bank investments, since insurance companies can provide guarantees that go well beyond what the banks offer.

In Canada, insurance products are the second most common planned gift, after bequests. Donations of life insurance policies and the residual remaining in insurance investments and annuities are the most common insurance gifts to charity. Some donors combine annuities and life insurance in a strategy commonly known as the "back-to-back" to create super-sized gifts for their charities. And you'll learn many other incredible ways to use insurance for philanthropic purposes in *Chapter 4*.

But first, let's explore the world of insurance. Insurance professionals use terminology that may leave you scratching your head. You can find more detailed definitions of those terms and many others in the glossary.

I should be clear that this chapter (and in fact, this book) does not provide an in-depth look at the nitty-gritty world of insurance. Insurance products change from year to year, and from company to company, and upon the printing of this book, such details would already be out of date. *This book is intended to provide a broad overview to gain functional literacy in the language of insurance.*

Common benefits offered by any insurance policy or product

Whether you purchase an insurance policy, an annuity to provide guaranteed retirement income, or invest your money in insurance company investment products like guaranteed investment certificates (GICs) or segregated funds, there are common benefits offered by insurance companies.

1. You will be required to assign a beneficiary to receive the death benefit from an insurance policy upon your passing, or to receive any residual funds remaining in your annuities or investments.

2. You can assign as many beneficiaries to each insurance product as you wish, and assign a percentage to each.

3. You can assign a back-up or contingent beneficiary to any policy. This allows policy owners to anticipate what may happen if the person assigned as beneficiary were to predecease the policyholder. There can be a string of contingent beneficiaries, if the policy owner wishes.

4. Monies going to your beneficiaries are not considered to be "bequests" nor are they part of your estate after your death. These funds are not subject to probate taxes nor can they be diminished by lawyer, accountant or executor fees.

5. Your beneficiaries will receive a cheque from your insurance company within two to three weeks of the insurance company being officially notified of your death and an

insurance claim is made.

6. Typically, any payments made to beneficiaries are in-contestable (other than by a dependent child or spouse), possibly creditor protected, and guaranteed by insurance companies.

7. Money invested in Canadian insurance companies is very safe. Canadian insurance companies are as highly regu-lated by Canadian federal government as Canadian banks. In fact, in some ways, investing your money in insurance company products are better than similar bank products because insurance companies provide their clients with guarantees that go well beyond what banks offer.

8. On some investment products like GICs, insurance com-panies may offer you a higher rate of return than banks.

Life Insurance

People (insureds/owners) purchase (get underwritten for) life insurance (insurance contracts) for many reasons. Most com-monly, people buy insurance to provide a spouse, children or other heirs (beneficiary/ies) with tax-free financial support in the form of a death benefit after the insured person dies. Insurance is also used to allow heirs to inherit more, by employing the death benefit to cover estate taxes.

Insurance is also purchased for the exclusive purpose of making a charitable donation. The insured can make the charity either a beneficiary of the policy's death benefit, or both the owner and beneficiary of the policy. This is explained in detail in *Chapter 4*.

Insurance policies can either be purchased to pay out a pre-determined fixed sum (a specified death benefit), or an amount (cash value) that will grow larger over the lifetime of the person who is insured.

The value of premiums paid on an insurance policy varies, depending on the person's gender, age and health. It costs less to insure women because they typically live longer than men. Usually people who are older and/or those who have some medical conditions will get less insurance for the same premium costs, compared to insurance policies purchased by younger and healthier people.

The cost of insurance can change weekly, and can vary dramatically from insurance company to company. There are also many ways to pay for life insurance. Typical ways include monthly payments for life or single annual payments. Some policies can become full funded (guaranteed to never lapse over the lifetime of the insured) by premiums made over a fixed number of years (called quick or short-pay policies). Some can even be fully funded in one payment.

Many types of life insurance policies accumulate a pool of cash within them known as a cash value or cash surrender value. Often policyholders never touch this cash but they have the option to use it in these ways:

1. Use the cash as an interest-bearing loan against their policy. Whatever amount that isn't repaid by the time they die is deducted from the policy's death benefit.

2. If the owner no longer needs the policy, he or she can collapse the policy and walk away with the cash.

3. Use the cash value to pay premiums. This can be known as premium offset or premium vacation. If there is sufficient cash value in a policy to guarantee that all premiums will be paid until the owner's death, the policy is considered fully funded or self sustaining.

Who can qualify to purchase life insurance

People as young as 15 days old can be insured. People usually can't be insured if they are over the age of 80 or 85 (depending on the province they live in, or the type of insurance they are applying for).

Some policies require applicants to undertake a basic medical examination to determine if they qualify for insurance (a process insurance advisors refer to as underwriting). This often means an insurance company sends a nurse out to the person's home. For a lower value policy, all that may be required is having blood pressure measured, giving a urine and/or blood sample, and answering "no" to the questions below. For higher-value policies (for example $1+ million), a blood sample and an electrocardiogram (ECG) may also be required, in addition to answering "no" to these questions:

Have you ever been diagnosed with one or more of the following?

- HIV, Acquired Immune Deficiency Disorder (AIDS) or AIDS-related complex
- Amyotrophic lateral sclerosis (ALS or Lou Gehrig's Disease)
- Congestive heart failure
- Cystic Fibrosis
- Huntington's Disease

Are you terminally ill or bedridden? "Terminally ill" means an illness, disease or condition diagnosed that would reasonably be expected to cause death usually within the next 12 months.

Typically, if someone answers "yes" to any of these questions, they cannot purchase insurance. However, some types of specialized and non-medical insurance have more liberal qualification rules. Non-medical policies are typically lower-value policies, or are only available to younger people.

How policies are paid off

Policy owners usually pay off policies in installments (premium payments), typically monthly or annually.

Some policies (often these are universal life policies) can be entirely paid up in one payment, or over a specific period of time set out in the insurance contract. With younger people, policies that can be paid off in 10 to 20 years are quite popular.

Other types of policies (permanent life insurance; whole life insurance) either require payments to be made regularly until the insured person dies, or the policy could be arranged to be paid in full in a specific number of years, such as 10 or 20. If these payments stop and the policy has not accumulated sufficient cash value to pay for some or all future premiums, the policy is cancelled (lapses). All the money paid into the policy is lost to the policyholder, and is retained by the insurance company. This is why experienced advisors who understand charitable giving through insurance will explore the benefits of quick-pay policies with their clients.

The death benefit of a life insurance policy is guaranteed by the insurance company. It will not be less than the amount outlined in the insurance contract. It may be larger, if a policy is chosen that has a cash value that grows over time.

Exposing the "magic" behind life insurance policies that grow in size over a donor's lifetime

These kinds of policies make excellent legacy gifts, since the premium payments donors pay for these policies may be significantly less than the size of the death benefit received by the charitable beneficiary of their policy. Some fundraisers have asked me how it is possible for insurance companies to offer policies that pay out much more than people pay into them.

It boils down to a concept called pooling. Let's say 500 people buy life insurance from one company. They've all bought insurance for their own reasons and are paying different amounts based on their age, health, size of policy, etc. All their premiums are pooled together by their insurance company.

Time passes and 100 people from this group realize that the reason for which they bought their life insurance policy is no longer valid. They stop paying their premiums and let their policies lapse. These premiums stay in the insurance company's pool with the ongoing premiums of those who are still insured.

Another 200 people from this group bought term insurance for a specific purpose, like paying off their mortgage if they die before their home is paid off. These people didn't die prematurely, paid off their mortgage, and cancel their insurance. Their premiums also stay in the pool.

The premiums paid on lapsed and cancelled term policies, plus all the funds coming in daily from insurance premiums, are invested in safe long-term investments like real estate or government bonds, which helps grow the size of the pot used to cover insurance payouts.

For the remaining 200 people who still are paying into their life insurance policy upon their death, their beneficiaries will get their share of this pool of money. So for example, that's why an insurance company can sell you a policy with a $100,000 benefit that might only cost you a total of $30,000 paid over the years.

Term Insurance

Policies specifically purchased to pay off debt like mortgages in case of unexpected financial hardship or premature death are known as term insurance. Payments are made for the lifetime of the mortgage loan.

After term insurance expires, it has no value. However, most term insurance can be converted all or in part into permanent life insurance prior to the policy's expiration date.

Insurance company investment products

Unlike buying life insurance, no medical evaluation is required of anyone who wishes to obtain any insurance company investment products. However, some products have age restrictions.

Insurance companies offer many of the same investment products you can purchase through banks, including variable annuities, Guaranteed Investment Certificates (GICs), segregated funds (like a mutual fund), Registered Education Savings Plans (RESPs), Registered Retirement Savings Plans (RRSPs), Registered Retirement Income Funds (RRIFs) and Tax-Free Savings Accounts (TFSAs).

They also sell guaranteed income products called annuities that provide guaranteed income for life.

All insurance investment products require the owner to assign a beneficiary to receive any residual funds remaining at the time of the owner's death. When charities are assigned as a beneficiary, they receive these funds within two to three weeks of the donor's executor making a claim to the insurance company.

There are billions of dollars in invested income in insurance companies. It's about time Canadian charities start suggesting that they would be happy to be named beneficiaries of these investments! It is so easy for a donor to understand and do.

Annuities

Annuities and variable annuities are used to provide people with life-long guaranteed retirement income. They are becoming more popular because of a common fear revealed in a 2010 poll done by the American Association of Retired People – more than three in five people between the ages of 44 and 75 revealed that running out of money before they die is a greater fear than dying. Annuities solve that problem. You may want to consider them for your own peace of mind!

In exchange for making a lump sum payment on an annuity to an insurance company, they offer you (the annuitant) set payments that return to you some of your capital, plus interest. The payment size will never decrease, and will continue even if you outlive the amount you paid for your annuity. When you purchase a life annuity, you can choose to receive income for the rest of your life. You can purchase a term annuity to provide income for any specified time period you choose. A term certain annuity includes a guarantee that income payments will be made for the full term, even if the annuitant dies before the term expires.

When you buy a prescribed annuity with non-registered funds — such as cash from chequing or savings accounts; bank GICs; funds resulting from the sale of stocks, bonds, property, etc. — taxes on your payments are low, since only the interest portion of your payment is taxable.

You can use registered savings to fund registered annuities — money you saved in registered retirement savings plans (RRSPs) or registered investment funds (RRIFs) —100% of your registered annuity payments are considered income and are fully taxed.

Couples or siblings can jointly purchase an annuity. When one passes away, payments continue for the rest of the survivor's life. Typically these annuity payments are lower because the annuity covers two lives.

Annuities are so popular because they often offer a higher rate of return than other investments. They also eliminate market risk, which provides a guaranteed pension to the annuitant. These are often suitable for those who can't afford to have fluctuating or negative income from savings invested in stocks, bonds and mutual funds.

Turn to *Chapter 4* for more about Charitable Gift Annuities, which donors can buy directly from some charities.

Chapter 4

THE BASICS
OF CHARITABLE GIVING
THROUGH INSURANCE

"Do your little bit of good where you are.
It is those little bits of good put together that
overwhelm the world."

— Desmond Tutu, South African Archbishop,
Activist & Nobel Peace Prize Winner (1931-)

What are the most common ways donors give using insurance?

In this chapter, you can read some examples of typical ways that people use insurance to further their philanthropic goals through fictional composite donor stories that illustrate how easy and effective making gifts of insurance can be. I'll also lead you through detailed how-to explanations that will help your charity better work with your donors who want to learn more about giving in this way.

You'll want to bookmark *Appendix 4*. In chart form, you've been given a handy "Fundraiser's Cheat Sheet" on using insurance for charitable giving.

Life Insurance

Donors have used life insurance to generate legacy gifts for generations. The mechanics behind giving in this way can change from country to country, since legal regulations surrounding insurance differ, and change from time to time. This book is written from a Canadian perspective, but includes many truths that are universal.

No matter what country you live in, there is a dizzying array of life insurance options, and they change from year to year. There are also a myriad of ways to pay for them, and the cost can change weekly.

I highly recommend that any donor considering an insurance gift, or any charity deciding to accept such gifts, consult an independent insurance broker who is comfortable in talking to their clients about their philanthropic goals, and can shop the entire market for the most appropriate product to meet individual needs. If you want your favourite broker or insurance agent to become an expert on charitable giving using insurance, direct them to companion of this book, *Ripple Effect: Growing your business with insurance and philanthropy*, written for financial advisors.

Donation of a fully funded, unneeded life insurance policy

Ghislaine Forest, President of the Delectable Edibles Bakeries empire, decides to name The Kids Can Bake Foundation as the beneficiary of a fully-funded, self-sustaining $500,000 life insurance policy she no longer needs. In case Ghislaine experiences a future family emergency, she wants the option of changing the beneficiary of her policy to a family member, so she assigns the Foundation as her policy's beneficiary, and retains the ownership of the policy.

In anticipation that the Foundation will receive the policy's death benefit, Ghislaine spoke with Foundation staff and arranged for the Foundation to endow the proceeds of her policy. Its annual interest will fund scholarships for promising bakers, given in the name of Ghislaine's late mother, Jeanne Sicotte, the founder of Delectable Edibles.

Ghislaine did not get charitable tax receipts for the premiums she continued to pay on her policy until her death. But when the Foundation became the beneficiary of her policy, the $500,000 charitable tax receipt sent to Ghislaine's estate generated a huge tax credit that allowed Ghislaine to leave an additional $250,000 to her children and grandchildren.

The key details

The most common ways donors use life insurance as a donation is to offer a charity an insurance policy they no longer need. For example, a mom buys life insurance to provide for her son if she passes away while he's still young, but Mom's still around and her son is now a self-sufficient adult.

An important distinction when evaluating such a gift is that the policy is fully funded (also called self-sustaining, paid-up, or on premium offset). This means that the donor has already made sufficient premium payments to date, which have accumulated sufficient cash value within the policy to pay all future premiums and keep the policy active until the death of the insured person.

Before accepting any policies, you'll first want a guarantee that a 'fully funded' policy will never lapse. Contact the insurance company that issued the policy and ask for an In-Force Illustration. This report will confirm the date the policy was issued, the quantity of premiums paid on that policy to date, the current accumulated cash value, if there are any further premium payments needed to fully fund the policy, and the projected death benefit in future years. I strongly recommend getting the help of an insurance professional to review the illustration with you before you accept any gifts of insurance policies.

If all is well, your charity will get the greatest value from such gifts if the donor transfers the **ownership** of his or her policy to your charity *and* names your charity as the **beneficiary**. This is a quick and simple procedure that involves the donor contacting their insurance company and completing one form. To bulletproof the ownership transfer, ensure your donor uses the legal name of your organization on the transfer form.

Once your charity becomes the owner and beneficiary of a permanent life policy, you must issue a charitable tax receipt to the donor for either the cash value or the policy's fair market value, as of the date of its transfer to your organization. The fair market value can be much higher than the cash value, and will probably fall between the amount of premiums paid into the policy and the value of its death benefit (or face value). You must employ an actuary to determine exactly what the fair market value is. Some charities pay the actuarial fee (which can be in the $2,000 range); other charities pay the fee and ask the donor to cover the cost by making a charitable donation equal to the value of the actuarial fee.

If the policy has a large accumulated cash value and your charity has urgent immediate funding needs, you can choose to collapse the policy and redeem the cash value.

If the policy's cash value is non-existent or small, and your organization can afford to wait for the gift until the insured person dies, then your charity will receive the full death benefit of the policy upon death of the donor – which is typically substantially more than the cash value alone.

Alternately, a life insurance policy donor may choose to only name your charity as **beneficiary** because he or she can benefit more from estate tax relief. Since the donor then retains the right to change the beneficiary of their policy at any time, you will have no claim on the policy (including any current cash value) unless the donor keeps your charity as the beneficiary until he or she passes away. If this is the case, your charity will receive the full value of the policy's death benefit, and will issue a charitable tax receipt to the donor's estate for that amount. In many cases, gifts of this type come as a surprise to your charity. If you have favoured advisors, you could ask them to encourage their clients to inform their charity about their intention to give a planned gift, so that they could together discuss any preferences the donor may have on how the gift is used, and if the donor would agree to any recognition of their gift intention for the purpose of inspiring others to do the same.

The "Dump and Run" – Donation of a life insurance policy that requires the charity to take over payment of premiums

"I don't need this policy any more," says your healthy 55-year-old donor. "It's worth a million dollars and I'd like to give it to you. All you need to do is pay the premiums on it until I die to get the $1 million."

Many donors think this is a very generous offer; most charities are quite uncomfortable with the offer because they can't afford to pay insurance premiums for decades, even if the payoff will be great. You have to consider that this donor might live for another 45 years. In addition, if the donor simply walks away from the charity and the gift, the charity may not learn when the donor passes away, which is necessary to claim the death benefit.

In some cases, donors aren't focused on the impact of their gift to charity – they only wish to release themselves of the burden of their insurance policy and get a tax receipt as an added bonus.

There will be others who do care about your cause, and they may truthfully argue that the total paid on donated policy's premiums, even if for decades, may well be only a fraction of the final generous death benefit the charity will receive.

In either case, if your charity decides not to accept this kind of policy (*read more about creating your own Gift Acceptance Policy in Chapter 8*), you should be sensitive to the donors offering this kind of gift and let them down gently, explaining that your charity simply doesn't have cash reserves necessary to pay premiums, maybe for decades.

Alternately, you can talk to the donor about the fact that you would have to collapse the policy, and that the donor can receive an immediate tax receipt for the policy's current fair market value. If the policy is at least five years old, it may still result in a generous donation based on the value of the premiums paid into it, plus the any additional accumulated cash value (if it is a policy that grows in value over time).

In some circumstances, accepting a policy that requires making ongoing payments may be a good investment for your charity.

Points to consider before accepting a life insurance gift

When deciding to accept a life insurance donation of a policy that requires your charity to take on its premium payments, consider the **age** and **health** of the donor:

For example: If a donor is 80+ and in failing health, and their policy is for $50,000 or more, your investment in paying their premiums may well be worth a relatively short wait for the resulting gift. You can further lower the risk of accepting a policy if it has a guaranteed death benefit, guaranteed cash value, fixed annual premiums, and your charity is named owner and beneficiary of the policy. Some charities have used creative ways to fund premiums including:

- Pooling monthly and payroll gifts from fundraising staff to pay premiums on a policy donated by very loyal, very elderly donor, who wanted the charity to benefit from the large policy, but who could no longer afford the premiums.

- Asking other loyal donors (who regularly make annual donations at least the size of the policy's annual premiums) to assist the charity in securing a significant gift by allowing the charity to dedicate this donor's gifts toward paying another person's donated policy premiums. If the donor agrees to cover these premiums, you would issue tax receipts to your loyal donor for all funds he or she donates to cover another's premiums.

- Using undesignated money held in a large endowment fund to pay the premiums. You may wish to consult with an actuary about the specific circumstances of this policy and its donor to predict if the rate of return is lucrative enough to treat the donated policy as an investment.

If your charity has decided to accept the offer of a known donor with clear charitable intent to become the new owner and beneficiary of a donated policy — and *you can guarantee that your charity will cover all remaining premiums until the donor dies* so the policy does not lapse — you can give the donor a charitable tax receipt for the policy's fair market value, as determined by an actuary, if the policy is a permanent life policy. Some charities cover the cost of the actuarial fee themselves, or they require donors to make an additional donation to cover the fee.

Important: If you offer a charitable tax receipt for the fair market value of a donated policy, and your charity lets the policy lapse (making the policy valueless), your charity can receive an intermediate sanction by the Canada Revenue Agency and be forced to pay a penalty for false receipting of the policy. So follow the best practices noted in this book to help your charity receive the greatest possible charitable benefits from gifts of insurance!

Even if a proposed donated policy seems bulletproof and you're willing to pay the premiums until the donor's death, it's always good practice to approach a trusted insurance or financial advisor and ask him or her to evaluate whether the policy is worth more in the long run than simply investing the estimated amount you'd have to pay in premiums. Advisors call this analysis a net present value calculation.

Another useful tool to evaluate the policy being offered is an in-force illustration generated by the insurance company that issued the policy. You can ask the potential donor to approach their insurance company and supply an illustration. If any of the following warning signs appear in an in-force illustration, it is probably a bad bet to accept these kinds of policies:

- Death benefit decreases in size as the person ages.

- No cash surrender value.

- Modified or graded premiums that will increase in amount in the future. This kind of policy is often purchased by a younger person who can't afford to pay full premiums right away but who anticipates higher earnings in the future. These policies offer low premiums for a specified number of years, and then increase substantially in a single year to the level they will remain.

- Year Renewal Term insurance (YRT; a.k.a. increasing term insurance or annual renewal term insurance). One-year term life insurance policy with premiums based on the owner's age and other risk factors. If the policyholder chooses to renew the insurance, their premiums increase with each annual renewal. YRT is especially attractive to younger people because of its initial low premiums and the payment of a death benefit to named beneficiaries if the policyholder passes away within the year term of the contract. Historically, YRT policies have proven to be poor insurance gifts to charity. The fact that the policy is literally a year term, requiring annual renewal, gives the product no sense of permanent obligation. Increasing premium payments also can quickly become unaffordable for donors, who typically let the policy lapse. Recently, YRT products have become more popular but their past dismal success rate as charitable gifts mean that you should not accept these products as donations.

If you use organizational funds to pay the remaining premiums on a gifted policy, it is important to know that the Canada Revenue Agency does not consider these payments to be a fundraising expense, nor do they count towards meeting your disbursement quota (the percentage of funds that must be dispensed from monies you raise). Similarly, CRA does not consider death benefits you receive from gifted policies to be fundraised income when your charity is calculating your disbursement quota.[4]

If the life insurance policy has a significant accumulated cash

4 CRA's Interpretation Bulletin No. IT-244R3 – *Gifts by Individuals of Life Insurance Policies as Charitable Donation.*

value, you can accept the policy after your charity is named its owner and beneficiary, collapse the policy, collect the cash value, and issue a tax receipt to the donor for that amount.

If your charity is seriously considering accepting such an offer and will assume the ownership of the policy and responsibility for the premiums, talk to the donor about the tax relief he or she expects to receive for the policy.

- Inform the donor that when your charity accepts ownership of the policy and becomes its beneficiary that the donor will not receive a tax receipt for the death benefit of the policy when he or she dies.

- Your donor wants estate tax relief, and offers a policy on which he or she will remain the owner, and will assign your charity as the beneficiary if your charity pays the premiums. **Decline the offer.** The donor can change the beneficiary of a policy at any time. It is never worth the risk to accept such an offer.

- The donor of a permanent life policy can accept a charitable tax receipt for the fair market value of the policy, as calculated by an actuary who weighs several factors including the donor's health and life expectancy. This will be for only a portion of the value of the death benefit, because all the potential costs of the premiums to be paid by the charity are deducted from the policy's value.

- The donor can receive a charitable tax receipt for the cash surrender value of the policy, which the charity will accept as a donation when it accepts ownership of the policy, makes the charity its beneficiary, then keeps or collapses the policy. You do not need to hire an actuary or pay any other fees to proceed in this way.

Donation of a life insurance policy purchased specifically to act as a philanthropic gift

Mary Scott is a healthy 50-year-old Ontarian, and a respected director in her company. She wants to use the multiplying power of life insurance to make a substantial gift to one of her favourite charities.

Mary buys a $50,000 permanent life insurance policy, chosen specifically because it can be paid up in any time frame she wishes. Since Mary is in her peak earning years, she decides to pay up the entire policy in five years. She names a favourite charity as the policy's owner and beneficiary. She then arranges a meeting with this charity, and instructs them to direct her policy's death benefit into their endowment fund, so she can support their good works in perpetuity.

Her monthly premiums are $350 a month (or $4,200 a year). Mary is delighted that the charitable tax receipts she gets for her premiums let her deduct about 41%** of their value from her annual income taxes.

Over five years, Mary pays $21,000 in premiums, but thanks to charitable tax credits worth $8,400, her real cost to purchase the $50,000 policy benefiting her charity is only $12,600.

After her policy is paid up, Mary is so thrilled by her ability to make a significant continuing impact on this charity's work that she purchases another policy benefiting another favourite charity!

*Note: The amount of the premium reflected in this example will not reflect everyone's personal circumstances. The value of premiums a person pays are based on his or her age, health, weight, occupation, the type and value of insurance policy chosen, and the time frame in which he or she wishes to pay its premiums.

**Canadian charitable tax credits vary from about 40 to 50%, depending on the province or territory a donor lives in. In Ontario, the tax credit is approximately 41%.

The key details

As you've read in *Chapter 1*, there are many outstanding benefits people receive from making a gift through life insurance.

The importance of getting advice from a knowledgeable and ethical advisor

It is critical that donors consult insurance advisors who put The needs of their clients first and foremost. This includes engaging them in conversations about their clients' philanthropic dreams and wishes. Some advisors are hesitant to have this conversation with clients because they are worried about decreasing the size of the assets they manage (and therefore their income) if their clients start giving substantial sums to charity. Advisors have to realize that in truth, if a client is inclined to make significant gifts to their favourite charities, the advisor can choose to be involved in the process or be left out of it.

The best advisors encourage and aid their clients to make gifts that can have the biggest impact on the work of their charity by using the financial methods that benefit both the donor and charity. The goodwill and trust that the advisor gains by helping their clients in this way is actually likely to lead to more business from their existing clients, and often from referrals including new business from the clients' like-minded family members and friends.

It is important for advisors to understand the methodologies of how insurance is best used for charitable giving, since it may help their clients give the most generous legacy gift possible to their charity, while generating increased estate tax relief that helps their clients also leave more to friends, family or other charities.

For example, advisors who don't understand the philosophy of charitable giving are likely to suggest donors purchase permanent policies that require premiums to be paid until the insured dies. This is often the advice donors receive because these policies offer the least expensive premiums. But in the end, these policies are often left to lapse and become worthless, and here's why.

Few donors give to the same charity for decades, until they die. As they grow older, their interests and priorities often change, leading them to shift their charitable giving to organizations that reflect their new goals. Or as they age, and health care costs grow while savings shrink, donations — including the premiums for a policy donated to a cause that is no longer top of mind — become a lower priority.

Savvy insurance advisors understand the psychology behind this behaviour and advise their clients to purchase policies that will fulfill the goals of both the donor and his or her charity. These advisors often direct donors to buy policies that are fully funded (and forever self-sustaining) by one payment – especially when their clients have experienced a cash windfall from an inheritance or real estate sale. Or, they can suggest guaranteed policies that will be funded over a defined period of time, like 10 years.

Good advisors try to direct donors towards policies that have a guaranteed death benefit or one that grows in value over the donor's lifetime, and/or a policy that accumulates a cash value.

They can also help donors take advantage of lower premiums offered by pay-for-life policies by suggesting a permanent payment strategy called a "back-to-back" (also see *Chapter 5*). Using this strategy, a donor purchases an annuity (more on this later in the chapter) whose monthly payments fund their gifted life insurance policy until they die, due to the annuity payments being directly deposited into the account from which insurance premiums are automatically deducted.

Finally, you should also understand how insurance agents

or brokers get compensated for selling any type of insurance product to clients – whether they are used as charitable gifts or not. Clients are not normally charged a fee for the work their agent does on their behalf; the cost of agent compensation/commission is built in to the cost of any insurance product. Commissions vary according to the type and value of insurance product sold. The most ethical agent will not push clients into purchasing products that offer agents higher commissions, but which will result in a less effective gift.

If you have favourite financial and/or insurance advisors who should learn industry best practices on giving through insurance, you may wish to buy them a copy of *Ripple Effect: Growing your business with insurance and philanthropy*, the sister book to this one for professional advisors, also written by this book's authors Jack Bergmans, CFP, and Marlena McCarthy.

Assigning a charity to be the owner and beneficiary of a new insurance policy

In this charitable arrangement, a donor buys life insurance and pays all the premiums on a policy whose death benefit will go to a charity assigned as owner and beneficiary of the policy. Donors often choose this option because they want tax relief from the premium payments during their lifetime.

Because the donor grants ownership of the policy to a registered charity, this charity considers all of the premium payments made by the donor as charitable gifts. Usually a charity will send the donor a tax receipt for the combined total of all premiums made over a calendar year. Charities learn the exact value of these payments by requesting a letter from the insurance company each January that verifies the value of premiums paid in the previous year.

If the donor misses any premium payments or stops paying premiums

The insurance company will notify the charity. If you know the donor is still alive and through your call or letter you learn that the donor is not able (or willing) to continue making future payments, you have four choices:

- You can terminate the policy, extract any cash value and put it to immediate use. Issue a tax receipt to the donor for all the premiums paid from the time you last sent him or her a receipt. The donor is not eligible to receive a charitable tax receipt on the value of the cash surrender value of the policy, since the donor assigned the charity to be the policy's owner.

- If the donated policy has an accumulated cash value, you can ask the insurance company if the policy has the option of being turned into a reduced paid-up policy. This will lower the death benefit of the policy, but no further premium payments will be required to keep the policy in force until the donor passes away. Taking this option may result in a final gift that is significantly greater than the current cash surrender value.

- If the circumstances surrounding this policy could be favourable for your charity — e.g. the donation could be very large, the policy payments are manageable, or there are limited payments due to the type of policy or the life expectancy of the annuitant — your charity may choose to continue to make the policy payments, or find another donor to do so on your behalf. This allows your organization to receive the policy's full death benefit, which will be significantly more than the cash surrender value.

- If you do nothing, the policy lapses and all the funds paid into the policy are kept by the insurance company. Nobody wins in this scenario except for the insurance company.

If a donor is concerned that the charity he or she assigns as owner and beneficiary may not be in existence upon his or her death, the donor can assign a contingent beneficiary to the policy. For example:

- In the case that <Legal Name of Charity> no longer exists at the time of my death, the beneficiary of my policy will be <Legal Name of Second Charity>.

If a donor is unsure of which charity should be the contingent beneficiary, he or she has the option of assigning the policy's ownership to a local community foundation, and supplying instructions to the foundation asking them to choose a worthy organization that has a similar mandate to the primary beneficiary, or to direct the policy's proceeds to a charity with another specified mandate altogether.

Donors should be advised to only assign one charitable owner for their gifted policy. Although it is possible to name two or more charities as co-owners of one gifted policy, it can create an accounting nightmare for the charities involved. If a donor really wishes to split the proceeds of a single policy, a good alternative is to name their local community foundation to be the policy's owner, and give instructions to the foundation on how his or her gift is to be divided. Or, a donor can be asked to contact their insurance company and request that their policy is split into separate policies, assigning one charity to each policy.

Assigning a charity to be the beneficiary (not the owner) of a new insurance policy

In this charitable arrangement, a donor buys life insurance and pays all the premiums on a policy whose death benefit will go to a charity assigned as its beneficiary. Donors often choose this option because they want the option of changing the beneficiary on their policy should family or emergency needs arise, or if they no longer wish that particular charity to receive their legacy gift.

This is also a preferred option if a donor knows their estate will incur a large tax bill from the liquidation of registered savings, securities, properties and other assets. A large charitable tax receipt will reduce or eliminate their estate taxes, allowing them the option to leave more to other charities or their loved ones.

If the charity is still the beneficiary of the policy at the time of the donor's death, the death benefit gets transferred to the charity within two to three weeks after an insurance claim is made on the policy. The charity then sends the donor's estate a tax receipt for the full value of the death benefit. The tax credits can be used against 100% of the donor's net income in the year of his or her death, and if they exceed the taxes owing, can also be used against 100% of the donor's net income in the year before his or her death.

It is possible for a charity to be named as the co-beneficiary of a split-value life insurance policy, with the charity receiving a percentage of the final death benefit, split with one or more other beneficiaries.

Insurance companies do not inform beneficiaries that they have been named as a beneficiary on an insurance policy. Similarly, if the donor stops making premium payments on this kind of policy, beneficiaries are not notified that this has happened.

If a donor stops making payments on such a policy, this policy may not lapse immediately – if the policy has accumulated any cash value, payments come from this cash until it is depleted. If the donor doesn't resume payments at that point, the policy will lapse and become worthless.

Donors often won't tell charities that they have assigned them to be a beneficiary of their insurance policy, especially if the donors suspect they may wish to change the beneficiary before they die.

Annuities

This insurance investment product can be called "The gift that gives back." Because annuities (or life annuities) allow a donor to be both philanthropic and receive guaranteed income for life, they are a popular way of making charitable gifts through insurance. Annuities can be gifted in three different ways.

1. **Self-Insured Charitable Gift Annuities**
    When donors assign a charity to be the beneficiary of any residue that remains in their annuity when they die, the insurance industry calls these *self*-insured charitable gift annuities.

    It is important to remember that if the donor lives long enough, he or she may outlive the capital initially invested in the annuity and therefore a charitable donation will not ensue.

    However, this should not discourage you from reminding your donors that they can assign a charity to be the beneficiary of their annuities. Any actuary will tell you that the law of averages indicates that the majority of people die before or around the average median age, which will likely result in your charity receiving a gift.

2. **Charitable Gift Annuities**
    Charitable gift annuities (a.k.a. reinsured charitable gift annuities or gift plus annuities) are offered by some Canadian charities – usually larger organizations with long-term mandates.

    In a contractual agreement, a donor (or a couple) gives the charity at least $10,000 in cash or securities, or as much as the donor wishes.

    A minimum of 20 per cent is retained by the charity as an immediate donation, and the charity issues a tax receipt to the donor for that amount.

    The balance of the funds is used by the charity to purchase

a prescribed annuity. To get the best value for their donors, charities should use an insurance broker to shop around for annuities with the highest income at that time, since rates of return can vary dramatically from company to company.

The charity becomes the owner and beneficiary of the annuity, and all annuity payments are set up to go to the donor. The donor pays tax only on the interest portion of their annuity income. For older donors, their annuity income may be entirely tax-free, giving them a return that could be up to 50% greater than they could realize with other types of investments or interest generated by savings.

Sample charitable gift annuity of $100,000 with $20,000 (20%) deducted as an immediate charitable donation

	Monthly Income[1]	Annual Income[1]	Annual Taxable Income	Gift & Receipt[2]	Annual Rate of Return[3]
Female, 77	$565.37	$6,784.44	$0	$20,000	6.78%
Male, 72	$544.54	$6,534.48	$0	$20,000	6.53%

[1] Annuity income is guaranteed for the rest of the annuitant's life, even if all capital invested has already been returned to annuitant.

[2] Value of charitable tax credit is between 40-50% of the gift, depending on where donor lives in Canada. Tax credits can be applied against present income taxes on up to 75% of annual income, or against income taxes for up to 5 years going forward.

[3] Annuity rates can change frequently. This rate is as of late December 2014.

3. The Back-to-Back Strategy

Annuity payments can be used to fund gifted insurance policies. You'll learn all about this in *Chapter 5*.

Chapter 5

GETTING CREATIVE
WITH CHARITABLE GIVING
THROUGH INSURANCE

"Apart from the ballot box,
philanthropy presents the one opportunity
the individual has to express his meaningful
choice over the direction in which our society
will progress."

— George G. Kirstein, American publisher

Are there other ways people can give using insurance?

Beyond the standard ways people use insurance, there are many insurance strategies that can help donors be more philanthropic than they could ever imagine.

When talking to your donors, keep these ideas in mind, especially if you discover they plan to give in ways that simply won't have the impact of effective insurance giving strategies.

The value of getting good financial advice: Integrating insurance to do good, and provide better care of loved ones

This example illustrates how some creative thinking allows a couple to do more, with the help of a joint last-to-die insurance policy.

. . . .

Mike and Samantha, Ontarians both aged 65, want to be generous to the university they both attended. At present, they have included in their Will a bequest of $75,000 to their university, which they have set aside in a tax-free savings account.

They also want to generously provide for their daughter Jane, who is a mother of four. They are bequeathing to her whatever will remain in their registered savings (RRSPs/RRIFs), but worry that taxes and probate-related fees will consume about half of these funds. Between them both, they currently hold about $350,000 in RRSPs.

After exploring their options with their financial advisor, they use their $75,000 in savings to purchase a $300,000 Universal Life joint-last-to-die life insurance policy, and assign Jane as its beneficiary.

They update their Will, removing the $75,000 donation. They replace it with a donation of the proceeds of whatever might remain in their registered funds, which are allowed to transfer directly to their university upon their death.

Mike and Samantha both pass away 20 years later. Because they both had employee pensions and other investments, their registered savings have only decreased by the minimum amount they were legally obliged to withdraw each year, and are worth $200,000.

If they had been transferred to their daughter as originally planned, Jane would have eventually received about $120,000, after tax and probate-related fees (legal and/or accounting) were settled. Instead, Jane now immediately receives the full tax-free death benefit of her parents' insurance policy, now worth about $378,000.

Their university receives $140,000, a donation almost two times greater than their original donation of $75,000. Their estate still must pay taxes on the RRIF but they are mostly offset by the charitable receipt their estate receives for their generous gift.

In the end, Mike and Samantha's university, and their daughter Jane, each receive almost four times as much as the couple originally planned, and in this simplified example, all of their taxes were offset by charitable tax receipts!

*Note: The amount of insurance purchased for $75,000 will vary according to the age and health each individual being insured. The value of registered funds upon death of their owners, after tax and probate-related fees, will vary from Canadian province to province.

Original Financial Plan	Revised Plan, Using Insurance
Charitable Gift	Charitable Gift
$75,000 from TFSAs	**$200,000** from RRIFs
Tax credits from donation $30,750	Income tax owed on RRIFs $82,000
	Tax credits from donation $82,000
Daughter's Inheritance	Daughter's Inheritance
Balance of RRIF **$200,000**	Insurance policy death benefit **$378,000**
Tax and probate-related fees ($82,000 + $4,500)	Tax and probate-related fees not applicable
Total inheritance **$113,500** received after probate is settled (**about 9 months later**)	Total inheritance **$378,000** received within **2-3 weeks** of insurance company receiving the insurance claim

. . . .

Marrying Annuities & Insurance: The Back-to-Back Strategy

Insurance and annuities are powerful financial tools. In the right situations, people can use a back-to-back strategy (also called insured annuities) to enhance after-tax income rather than suffer lifestyle constraints from low interest rates, while also providing generous bequests to charity and their heirs. This example shows how this can be done.

. . . .

Eva is a retired 65-year-old Canadian widow and mother of two living in a rental apartment in Calgary, Alberta. Eva has three key goals in life:

- To live comfortably.
- To leave her children residual funds from her estate.
- To donate generously to her favourite charity.

Eva is living off Old Age Security and Canada Pension Plan funds, deductions from RRIF savings currently worth $150,000, and $1,836 per year in after-tax income made on

2.7% interest earned on $100,000 in non-registered GICs. Having an income of less than $39,000 a year, Eva's tax rate is 22%.

Eva has assigned her charity as the beneficiary of the residue of her RRIF, and has bequeathed whatever is left of her GIC savings to her children.

But Eva's interest income is low and the cost of living in Calgary is going up. Eva feels she is eating too quickly into her RRIF to pay her bills, and worries she can't achieve any of her goals if she outlives her money.

She goes to her financial advisor to ask him if there is a better way for her to manage her finances and to improve her income without increasing her investment risk. He guides her through some highly beneficial strategic changes.

- Eva purchases a $100,000 whole life insurance policy that will grow in value over time, and assigns her children as its co-beneficiaries. Her annual premiums are $2,815.

- Using her $100,000 in GICs, Eva purchases an annuity. Her insurance broker ensures she gets the highest rate of return at that time. Although Eva no longer retains access to this capital, her annuity guarantees her after-tax income of $5,707 annually, for life.

- Eva uses $2,694 from her annual payments to cover her insurance premiums. She's thrilled this will guarantee her children an inheritance of a minimum of $50,000 each. She also bequeaths any tax refunds generated by her charitable tax credits to her children.

- To help Eva live more comfortably, she now has $2,897 in after-tax dollars from her annuity payment. Because of this increased income, Eva reduces her RRIF payments, further reducing her income tax.

Eva peacefully passes away, 20 years later, at age 85.

This chart allows you to see how Eva's Back-to-Back Strategy has allowed her to achieve her life's goals.

Eva's original financial plan	Eva's new back-To-back strategy
Eva's annual income	**Eva's annual income**
From $100,000 GIC earning 2.7% **$2,700**	From $100,000 annuity **$5,707**
Income tax payable at 22% ($594)	Life Insurance premium ($2,694)
	Income tax paid on taxable amount of annuity @22% ($115.61)
Eva's net GIC income $2,106	**Eva's net annuity income $2,897.39**
Eva's estate	**Eva's estate**
Charitable legacy gift	**Charitable legacy gift**
Donation of RRIF **$80,000**	Donation of RRIF **$100,000**
Charitable tax credits **$40,000**	Charitable tax credits **$50,000**
Eva's estate taxes	**Eva's estate taxes**
Income tax on RRIF ($25,600)	Income tax on RRIF ($28,650)
Minus tax credits from donation ($40,000)	Minus tax credits from donation ($50,000)
Income tax owed $0	Income tax owed $0
Probate-related fees **($5,000)**	Probate-related fees **$0**
Tax credit balance of $14,400 generates a refund of $5,760 from previous year's taxes	**Tax credit balance of $21,350 generates a refund of $8,580 from previous year's taxes**
Eva's bequest to her children	**Eva's bequest to her children**
GIC residue $100,000	Life insurance policy (value after 20 yrs.) $130,000 (tax free)
Minus probate-related fees ($5,000), plus $5,760 tax refund from previous year (due to charitable tax credits)	Plus $8,580 tax refund from previous year (due to charitable tax credits)
Total bequest to children $100,760	**Total bequest to children $138,580**

Because Eva's money was simply rearranged with the help of her financial advisor, at no additional cost she can give significantly more to charity, leave more to her kids, and enjoy the comfort of having a higher annual income!

Note: *In this example, Eva's annuity income was determined based on the best rates available in December 2014, and a prediction of Eva's lifespan using mortality tables. As an Alberta resident, Eva's charitable tax credit is almost 50%; tax credits vary from province to province. This example shows how it is possible that a large charitable tax receipt could significantly reduce or eliminate taxes owing on the estate, but depending on the value of the donation and estate, this may not the be case for every individual. However, if charitable tax credits are greater than all taxes owed in a donor's terminal year, the unused balance can be applied to recover taxes paid in the year prior to the donor's passing - which provides another opportunity to pass on more to loved ones and charities.*

Upsizing a bequest by using insurance

If you discover you have a donor who has already set aside a bequest for your organization in liquid, non-registered assets (like cash, T-Bills, GICs), they can often increase the size of their legacy gift by transferring these funds into a life insurance policy.

There are policies available that both grow in size over the donor's lifetime, and can be paid off in as little as one payment. By making this change, their final gift will most likely be larger than the amount originally invested in the insurance policy. The donation will not be reduced by taxes, is not subject to probate, will come to your charity within two to three weeks of the insurance company receiving the donor's death, and is almost impossible to contest (other than by a dependent spouse or child).

Marrying gifts of securities and insurance to generate a large legacy gift

Donations of appreciated securities are a very popular giving option for Canadians because the donor does not have to pay capital gains tax on these securities. If securities donors are insurable, they could turn their gift into a much larger legacy gift. They purchase a quick-pay life insurance policy, assigning their charity as its owner and beneficiary, and also donate a gift of securities of sufficient size to cover all the insurance policy's premiums.

Gifts of Segregated Funds

Segregated funds are the insurance world's version of mutual funds. They offer potential investment growth and guarantee that their value at maturity will never drop below the principal amount invested, even if the value of the products held within the fund drops. So for example, if your donor assigns your charity as beneficiary of a segregated fund initially worth $50,000, it will still generate a $50,000 donation to your charity if the market crashes and the investments within the fund are only worth $35,000. If the value of the invested funds increases to more than $50,000, then your donation will be larger, reflecting the fund's growth. In contrast, if the value of a mutual fund donated through a Will is depressed at the time of the donor's death, your charity's gift will be eroded, and it is also decreased by the estate tax owed on the fund.

Increasing a legacy gift using insured GIC

If your donor already has their bequest set aside in a Guaranteed Investment Certificate (GIC) in a bank, he or she can offer you a faster and somewhat larger gift by simply transferring the funds in the GIC (upon maturity) into an insurance company GIC. Not only do insurance company GICs typically offer higher interest rates, donors can specifically assign the beneficiary of these insured GICs to your organization, making the donation virtually incontestable. Although the donor's estate still must pay taxes on interest earned in the GIC during the donor's lifetime, these taxes will be offset by the charitable tax receipt issued to the estate. In addition, the donation of an insured GIC occurs outside of the donor's estate, so the gift won't be reduced by probate taxes, and lawyers' and executors' fees, as would a gift made through the donor's Will. Best of all, when your charity is the beneficiary of an insured GIC, the gift will come directly to your organization within two to three weeks of the insurance company receiving the donor's death certificate and an insurance claim form.

Assigning a charity to be a contingent beneficiary to a policy

Those who need their insurance policies to provide financial security for their family members can still possibly be philanthropic by naming a charity as a contingent beneficiary on their insurance policy, to receive a portion or all of the death benefit should those named as beneficiaries be no longer alive when the policy owner dies.

Assigning a charity to be co-beneficiary to a policy

A donor can divide the proceeds from an insurance policy or possible residue from insurance products to more than one beneficiary. For example, a parent could name both their child and a charity to be co-beneficiaries of one policy. The policy owner must assign what percentage each beneficiary receives.

Assigning a charity to be the irrevocable beneficiary of a policy or insurance product

If a donor wants to ensure a charity receives the proceeds from an insurance policy or possible residue from insurance products, he or she can name a charity as an irrevocable beneficiary. This does not mean that the beneficiary cannot be changed before the death of the policy owner. However, it can only be changed with the consent of the charity named as irrevocable beneficiary. Usually charities will not want to give up their beneficiary status. But if the charity is about to fulfill its mission and be terminated, it can permit the donor to change the beneficiary, perhaps to another charity with a similar mandate.

Being uninsurable due to their health or age is not a barrier to buying life insurance

If a donor's best way to leave the biggest legacy possible is to purchase an insurance policy and they are uninsurable due to their age or health, he or she can purchase a policy that insures the life of a loved one (like a spouse or child) who is insurable.

For couples who want to give even more

A Joint Last-to-Die life insurance policy insures the lives of both members of the pair, which can include siblings or close friends. This kind of policy can offer lower premiums and larger death benefits to charitable beneficiaries, and is paid on the death of the final surviving member.

For couples who want to leave an enduring legacy through a named endowment

The cheaper cost of premiums on joint-last-to-die 'quick-pay' policies allows couples of modest income to leave a memorable and enduring legacy. For example, a couple who are 50 years old and non-smokers in good health can pay premiums of about $150 a month on a policy that may become self-sustaining in 10 years, and leave a charity a $50,000 endowment, or possibly more, if their policy is one that grows over the lifetime of the donor. By naming their charity the owner and beneficiary of the policy, the couple will receive tax receipts for all premium payments, giving them tax credits that reduce the cost of their monthly payments by 40 to 50% (depending where in Canada they live). In the end, the net amount they contribute to their policy is between $6,000 and $7,000 to generate a $50,000 gift! After their policy is fully funded, these donors can be encouraged to add to their endowment fund by making annual gifts, continue to direct monthly donations to their endowment, or can purchase another quick-pay policy.

For donors who wish to honour loved ones forever

A legacy gift of an insurance policy or directing to charity the proceeds from any insurance product can become a named endowment fund, which can be used as a named annual student award or in other ways to keep the loved one's memory alive.

For those who want their gift to benefit their charity in perpetuity

For charities with mandates that have no end in sight, donors can help them in perpetuity by arranging in advance to endow their legacy gift. They can create their endowed fund with annual gifts, and top it up with the proceeds of an insurance policy, leaving a larger annual gift in perpetuity.

For major givers wanting to have an even bigger impact

They can channel the tax savings they gain from their annual donations into funding a gift of life insurance. For example, a $20,000 annual gift from a 60-year-old female might generate a $9,000 tax credit. If this tax savings were channeled for 10 years into a participating life policy that becomes self-sustaining after 10 years, the donor would leverage their tax savings into a $175,000 legacy gift that may continue to grow in value over time.

For people who don't want the money paid into term insurance to go to waste

Many people buy term insurance that will pay off large loans like mortgages in the event that they die an untimely death.

This ensures that their loved ones aren't burdened with unexpected debt. Almost all term insurance contracts contain the right to be converted into a permanent policy, which can present a gifting opportunity. One ideal solution is for the policy owner to assign a charity to be the policy's owner and beneficiary, and add enough funds to the policy to ensure it is fully funded.

For major donors making multi-year capital pledges

They can guarantee that they will have the capacity to fulfill their pledge by buying a term insurance policy for the length of their pledge. If the insurance is not needed to fulfill the pledge, the donor can convert the term insurance into a fully-funded permanent life policy, and help their charity in an even greater way.

For those with existing insurance policies who cannot afford to purchase a new policy specifically to use as a legacy gift

On an existing insurance policy, they can name a charity as a contingent beneficiary, should the current beneficiary of their policy predecease the donor.

For donors concerned that a large charitable gift will affect the amount that they can leave to their heirs

An insurance policy can be purchased as a wealth replacement tool to offset their legacy gift. A donor can purchase a policy that pays out the same amount as their bequest or major gift, and name their loved ones as beneficiaries. The donor can use the tax refunds resulting from their donations to help pay insurance premiums.

For donors not interested in having a Will

In 2012, a survey done by the Lawyer's Professional Indemnity Company revealed that 56% of Canadians do not have a signed

Will. They simply may never have gotten around to creating a Will, or have specific reasons for not wanting to have a Will. Some believe that informal instructions given to family members such as "After I die, give my GIC to ABC Charity" is sufficient to leave a legacy gift.

Unfortunately, when a Canadian dies intestate (without a Will), the government of province they live in becomes the executor and follows defined regulations for the dispensation of an estate, which includes paying debtors then splitting the remainder between a spouse, children or closest relatives. The province doesn't recognize nor act on informal instruction on giving to charities.

Insurance products can be used to help donors who don't have a Will to guarantee that a gift goes to their charity. For example, a GIC held in a bank or trust company can be shifted into an insurance company GIC and the individual can assign a charity to be its beneficiary. Similarly, a person can make a charity the beneficiary of an existing life insurance policy.

When a donor dies intestate, he or she will not have an executor. If you are aware that your charity has been named as beneficiary on any kind of insurance product or policy, and you learn that the donor has passed away, you must obtain a death certificate from the office of the Attorney General and send it to the insurance company to claim your donation.

How corporations can benefit from gifts of life insurance

There are many insurance strategies that help businesses to be good corporate citizens – a practice that is proven to generate more customer loyalty and generate new business.

According to the 2012 Edelman goodpurpose® 2012 study, analyzing the behaviour of 8,000 consumers in 16 markets around the world, 87% of global consumers believe that business should put at least equal weight on society's interests as on business interests; *73% would switch brands if a different brand of similar quality supported a good cause; and 71% would help to promote a company's products and services if that company stands behind the work of a good cause.*

The following is just one example of how a corporation can use insurance to be seen as a good corporate citizen.

Buying an insurance policy on the principal shareholder

A privately-owned corporation can buy a life insurance policy on the life of the principal shareholder, with the corporation being the beneficiary of the death benefit. When the shareholder dies, the proceeds are used by the corporation to make a tax-deductible contribution to the charity.

This strategy has different advantages. Because the corporation owns the policy, it can pay the policy with **pre-tax income**, making its purchase more cost-effective than if the shareholder purchases a policy on his own life (and names the charity as beneficiary), since the individual's premiums are paid from **after-tax funds**.

Also, corporations can use the charitable tax receipt to reduce 75% of their taxable income in the year the donation is made, and make use of unused credits to reduce their taxes for up to five subsequent years.

Chapter 6

FINDING THE IDEAL
INSURANCE DONORS

"Never doubt that a small group
of thoughtful, committed citizens
can change the world.
Indeed, it is the only thing that ever has."

— Margaret Mead, American cultural
anthropologist, author and speaker

How can I identify a donor who can benefit from giving through insurance?

Giving through insurance isn't for everyone. But it may be accessible for more people than you think. Take fundraiser and former financial advisor Sandra Mimic as an example.

....

Sandra Mimic's university education had a profound effect on her. It added meaning and depth to her life, and led her towards a successful career as a financial advisor and insurance specialist.

Five years after Sandra graduated from Okanagan University College, the school was transformed into the Okanagan campus of the prestigious University of British Columbia (UBC).

Impressed by how this change would benefit post-secondary students and the community, Sandra joined a UBC volunteer committee to promote the changeover and to raise money to endow a bursary fund for students attending UBC's Okanagan campus.

One of the committee members, a UBC Alumni Relations Manager, was part of the committee, and reminded fellow committee members that they too could contribute to the student bursary fund. Acting on this gentle nudge, Sandra began to consider how she could make a heartfelt donation with long-lasting impact. Drawing on her financial background, she began to consider her own circumstances to determine what kind of gift would give her the most bang for her buck.

At that time, Sandra was 35. She was raising a family and had a large mortgage.

She had recently purchased insurance to protect her family, if calamity struck. This experience led her to explore using insurance to make her gift. Being a healthy non-smoker, she calculated that a $50,000 policy — to be paid off over 30 years — had manageable $30-a-month premiums.

So working in conjunction with a UBC Planned Giving Officer, she purchased the policy and signed an agreement with the university that specified that she was assigning UBC to be the policy owner. Further written instructions ensure that Sandra's legacy gift will be designated to the student bursary fund.

Because UBC is the policy owner, they send Sandra one charitable tax receipt each year for her combined annual premium payments, generating a tax credit that reduces Sandra's real premium cost to about $18.

Says Sandra, "Making a gift using insurance was a no-brainer. In the end, it will cost me about $6,400 to give a gift of $50,000. I also enjoy staying connected to UBC by being a member of their Legacy Society."

Sandra's experience with fundraising, and with making her own gift inspired Sandra to make a career change. She followed her heart and became a Planned Giving Officer with UBC.

Today, Sandra fulfills the dreams of children with life-threatening illnesses in her role as Major and Planned Giving Officer for The Children's Wish Foundation of Canada, and she is giving back to her organization, using insurance in a different way.

"My employee benefits include group life insurance coverage. Since I already have lots of life insurance to protect my loved ones, I named Children's Wish to be the beneficiary of my group insurance. If I leave this position, I can convert the insurance into permanent insurance to ensure I'll be fulfilling children's wishes, even after I've passed away."

Sandra reflects, "As a financial advisor, I loved helping my clients meet both their financial and philanthropic goals. As a fundraiser, my heart is touched every day as I help donors' spirits soar through carefully planned donations that brighten the lives of children with serious and life-threatening illnesses."

Profiles of ideal insurance donors

- **Thrifty** people who like the idea of their donation being significantly multiplied by insurance, and/or those looking for ways to lower their annual or estate taxes.

- **Philanthropically-minded** donors who wish to have a long-term effect on your charity, and who do not need to see the effect of a significant gift whose impact occurs after they pass away.

- **Detail-oriented planners**, who appreciate that their legacy gift is guaranteed to be whatever size they wish (or perhaps even more), even if they must deplete all of their assets during their lifetime.

- People who **want to make their executor's job easier.**

- **Parents** concerned their children might challenge a traditional bequest, in an attempt to gain a larger inheritance.

- **Affluent parents** who are concerned that bequeathing all their wealth to their children will tempt the kids to do nothing with their lives.

- **Older individuals** who have experienced the death of parents, family or friends, have come to terms with their own mortality, and want to put their affairs in order.

- **Family-focused** people who want to be very philanthropic, but are reluctant to make a bequest because it will erode the value of their estate and force them to leave less to their family.

Other traits of potential insurance donors

Anyone who owns existing insurance policies, annuities, or any investments held in insurance companies.

People usually assign a loved one to be the beneficiary of insurance products to provide financial security to those people after they are gone. Owners of existing insurance policies can name a charity as a contingent beneficiary, should those named as beneficiaries predecease them.

Childless individuals/couples who have done well financially, or whose children are well off.

This includes gay and lesbian individuals and couples, older women who have never married and who prefer the title "Miss", and people with no other heirs.

Donors capable of giving $200+ a month to pay off a time-limited insurance policy.

Time-limited short-pay policies are pricier than those with premiums that must be paid until death. Yet those who can afford a monthly payment of $200 or more can purchase a policy that is fully funded in five to ten years, which will leave your organization with a legacy gift that is significantly greater than their total premium payments. These donors can also benefit from substantial tax credits either on their premiums or their legacy gift, which reduces the real amount they'll pay for their policy by 40 to 50%.

Donors who have made single cash gifts between $100 and $5,000.

This would not include donors whose only donations of this size are gifts in kind, in memoriam or tribute donations, event sponsorships, purchases of lottery tickets, silent auction items, or charity merchandise.

Donors who support your organization in many different ways.

If donors make substantial single cash gifts, and also give in several other ways, including attending events, buying lottery or raffle tickets, making in memoriam or tribute gifts, etc., then this consistent display of loyalty makes them potential insurance givers.

30-somethings very passionate about your cause.
For a few hundred dollars a year paid over ten years on a per-manent life insurance policy, younger people can make a gift of a fully-funded life insurance policy that is of a significant size, is guaranteed, and that they can be proud to call their own. Canadian donors may also qualify for the First-Time Donor Super Credit, if they make their gift before December 31, 2017.

People between the ages of 40 - 80.
An ideal target is middle to upper income donors in the 40-55 age group in their peak earning years, who are largely debt-free, with very good cash flow. Look for those who have done very well in their careers or have come into significant money at a younger age. The age of 80 is an upper maximum to give using life insurance because most insurance companies won't insure people older than this.

Loyal donors who have given consistently over the last 3 years.
This is a good marker. Yet the length of time a donor needs to give to be considered a good prospect is a judgment call. It is sometimes possible for people to become very passionate about a charity's work very quickly if they have a close personal connection to your cause.

People who can purchase life insurance because they can answer "no" to these health-related questions:

1. Have you ever been diagnosed with one or more of the following?
   - HIV, Acquired Immune Deficiency Disorder (AIDS) or AIDS-related complex
   - Amyotrophic lateral sclerosis ("ALS" or Lou Gehrig's Disease)
   - Congestive heart failure

- Cystic Fibrosis
- Huntington's Disease

2. Are you terminally ill or bedridden? "Terminally ill" means an illness, disease or condition diagnosed that would reasonably be expected to cause death within the next 24 months.

Please note that health and age are not factors in buying any insurance product other than life insurance!

Donors who have received a large capital gain from the sale of a business.

Large windfalls can result in large tax bills. Gifts of insurance can offer people significant, immediate tax relief if they use some of the windfall to purchase an insurance policy and name your charity as the owner and beneficiary. Policies can be purchased in one payment and provide them with tax credits of between 40-50% of the amount of that payment. The policy will also provide your charity with a gift that can be significantly larger than the amount paid by the donor.

Donors who have included a bequest to your organization in their Will.

If they have already set aside the funds for this gift, a few strategic financial shifts — like using these funds to buy an insurance policy — can result in a much bigger gift, significant tax savings for the donor, and the ability to leave more to their heirs. And don't forget that unlike bequests, insurance gifts go immediately to your organization, are not subject to probate-related fees, and are virtually incontestable.

People with savings in bank GICs or mutual funds.

Insurance companies offer GICs and segregated funds that are almost identical to bank products, but have two distinct advantages: GICs usually offer a higher rate of interest, and segregated funds have guarantees that the death benefit will never be lower than the principal originally invested, even if the value of funds inside them has dropped. Both products allow the owner to assign a beneficiary to receive any residual funds after the owner passes away. By shifting bank GICs and mutual funds into insurance products, your donor can make your charity their beneficiary, and your charity will get their gift within two to three weeks of making an insurance claim.

Donors who want to make a significant gift but won't because they are worried about having enough funds to live on until they die.

Many seniors have legitimate concerns about outliving their money. They may be concerned about stretching their savings and may be worried about their current investments. Many are turning to annuities and variable annuities to offer them a higher rate of return and guaranteed income for the rest of their life, even if they outlive the capital invested. Annuities can allow your donor to live in comfort, and possibly still make a donation by assigning your organization as a beneficiary of any capital remaining in the annuity when they die.

People with fully funded life insurance policies originally purchased for reasons that no longer exist.

Many parents buy insurance policies to care for their children, in the event that they die prematurely. Later, these parents find themselves with grown children doing well, and a life insurance policy that now has no purpose. Other people purchase insurance to support the growth of their own business, and their success has eliminated the need for their policy. These are ideal gifting opportunities. Changing the ownership and/or beneficiary of such a policy simply requires completing and returning one form to the insurance company that issued the policy.

People who purchased mortgage insurance, and will soon be retiring their mortgage.

Some types of term insurance purchased for purposes like this can be converted into permanent insurance before the policy owner reaches a certain age (as specified by the individual policy). The permanent policy can then be gifted to charity.

Childless people whose company offers them group life insurance coverage.
These individuals can name a charity as the beneficiary of their death benefits.

Donors who are 71+ years old who don't need the income that they must now annually withdraw from their RRIF.
People who have registered retirement savings (RRSPs) must convert them into Registered Retirement Income Funds (RRIFs) no later than the end of the year in which they turn 71. RRIFs require that the owner withdraws at least a minimum percentage of their value each year, which becomes taxable income. People who have other savings or pensions to draw from may not need RRIF income, and can reduce their taxes **and** be charitable by:

- buying a single pay life insurance policy with their net RRIF proceeds, after taxes are deducted (if they are insurable), and achieve immediate tax relief by assigning the charity as owner and beneficiary of the policy, or receive estate tax relief by assigning a charity as the beneficiary.

- transferring the RRIF into an annuity and have the guaranteed annual annuity payments go to charity for ongoing tax relief, and estate tax relief by assigning a charity as beneficiary of any residual annuity funds upon the death of the annuity's owner.

Financial advisors, insurance agents or brokers, and accountants.
These individuals understand the value of using insurance in financial and estate planning, are likely to use insurance themselves and promote it to their clients.

Traits of people who are less likely to make gifts of insurance

Certain types of people are not eligible to purchase new life insurance policies; others may not have the ability or desire to support your charity in this way.

However, any person who already owns life insurance, annuities or any other investments in insurance companies can still make your charity the beneficiary of a life insurance policy, or name your charity as beneficiary to receive the residue of funds remaining in their annuities or investments. Giving in this way can be appealing to:

i. Those for whom it is very difficult and/or impossible to purchase new life insurance policies:

- people over the age of 80
- people in ill health (terminally ill, have HIV or AIDS, ALS, congestive heart failure, Huntington's disease, cystic fibrosis)

ii. Cash-poor donors who have told you they have left you a bequest, to be funded by the liquidation of assets in their estate upon their death.

iii. Donors whose only support of your charity is through:

- In memoriam/In celebration donors. *Exception: person who has made 3 or more of these gifts*
- Lottery/raffle ticket purchasers
- Auction donor/buyer

iv. Gift in kind donor

v. Event sponsor or event attendee

vi. Purchasers of charity merchandise (cards, calendars, mugs, etc.)

Chapter 7

PROMOTING
GIFTS OF INSURANCE

"Fundraising is the gentle art
of teaching the joy of giving."

— Henry A. (Hank) Rosso,
founder of fundraising schools in U.S.A. and
author of *Achieving Excellence in Fundraising*

How can I inform donors that giving through insurance is an option?

Everyone knows what insurance is. Few know that it can be a very powerful way to support their favourite charities. Even fewer know how to use insurance effectively to be philanthropic.

Let's face it – giving through insurance can be complicated. That's probably why you bought this book!

Because gifts of insurance can be very lucrative for your charity, it is worth promoting in a variety of ways. Like any type of fundraising, you must raise awareness first by getting the word out in as many ways as possible, using language and examples that are easy to understand.

Overall, I'd suggest that the most effective way to help donors determine if insurance is right for them is to first let them know that giving through insurance is possible. Subsequently, effective insurance gifts will most likely come from one-on-one conversations between donors and gift planners and/or financial advisors, who can learn more about the donor's personal circumstances and help the donor determine if giving through insurance is right for them.

Wording you can use to promote gifts of insurance

Here is suggested wording to promote the existence and benefits of insurance giving on your website, in a newsletter article, on a Gifts of Insurance fact sheet, and in a brochure on legacy giving or gifts of insurance.

❖ ❖ ❖

Gifts of Insurance

By using the multiplying power of gifts of life insurance and the financial security and tax advantages of annuities, you can be more generous than you imagined you could be.

Donations of insurance offer you several unique advantages. They occur outside of your estate, meaning your legacy gift will not be reduced by taxes or fees, will not affect the inheritance of your loved ones, and will come to your charitable beneficiary within two to three weeks after your executor has officially informed your insurance company of your passing.

There are many ways to use insurance products to your advantage.

1. **Donate a fully-funded life insurance policy that you no longer need.** By making *<legal name of charity>* the owner and beneficiary of a permanent policy, you will gain immediate tax relief from our charitable tax receipt for the fair market value of your policy. Or, if your estate can use tax relief generated by your policy's death benefit, name our charity the beneficiary or irrevocable beneficiary of your policy.

2. **Purchase a new life insurance policy specifically for the purpose of making a charitable gift.** We recommend purchasing a policy that can be fully paid off in a specific time period of your choosing, so you are not burdened with premiums in your later years. If you make your charity the *owner and beneficiary* of the policy, you will receive an annual tax receipt for the value of the premiums you have paid. Or, if your policy names our charity the *beneficiary* or *irrevocable beneficiary* of your policy, your estate will receive a tax receipt for the full value of the policy's death benefit, which will reduce estate taxes and allow you to leave more to your heirs.

3. **Name our charity as the beneficiary (or one of two or more beneficiaries) of any investment products you hold**

in insurance companies including annuities, variable annuities, segregated funds, GICs, RRSPs and RRIFs. Upon your passing, we become the beneficiary of any residual funds in your insured investments, for which we will issue your estate a charitable tax receipt, which will help to offset any taxes owing on donated funds held in registered accounts.

4. **If you have already set aside funds to donate to <*legal name of charity*> through your Will**, and they are currently invested in GICs, savings bonds, T-bills or other cash assets, you can shift these funds into identical insurance products and name our charity as the owner and/or beneficiary of any residual funds. This takes your donation out of your estate and protects it from being reduced by probate taxes and related fees. Or better yet, use these funds to fully fund a life insurance policy, and generate a much larger legacy gift.

To avoid any misunderstandings when assigning a charity as a beneficiary to insurance products, please use our full legal name and address: <*insert correct legal name and address.*>

For more information, please contact <*insert specific name, phone number and email address.*>

❖ ❖ ❖

Here's another idea: Use a real-life story as an example of insurance giving

If you are aware of any person who has assigned your charity as the beneficiary of a gift of insurance — whether it be one of your donors, volunteers, staff members, or board members — write up his or her story and include it in your newsletter, on the back of your gifts of insurance fact sheet, and/or use a short quote on your website and in your legacy or insurance giving brochure.

The story need not be a biography; it only needs to answer two questions: why does the donor give to your charity, and why did he or she choose to give through a gift of insurance.

Direct mail appeals and mass promotional campaigns

Mass mailings and large public pushes to encourage people to make gifts of insurance (especially using expensive one-size-fits-all life insurance policies in which every donor qualifies) usually result in either little interest, or gifts that have a higher risk of failure. Insurance giving is most effective when it is tailored to a person's individual circumstances, which can emerge in conversations with a gift planner and/or a financial advisor.

However, if your organization does annual mailings to selected donors to promote legacy giving, you can use a donor who has made a gift of insurance to sign the letter. Make sure the information in the package doesn't exclusively focus on making gifts of insurance and also promotes gifts made through the Will.

You can also include a checkbox mentioning gifts of insurance on the Legacy Giving portion of reply forms that go with regular direct mail appeals, below gifts of bequests.

When people ask for more information, ideally they should get a call. Re-read the parts of this book you need to keep the topic top of mind before you phone the donor. If they request more information by mail, have a fact sheet ready, then make a follow-up call. If they feel the need to speak with a financial advisor and don't have one, you can offer them a list of advisors whom your charity trusts for them to choose from.

Talk to donors

Keep insurance giving in mind when speaking with major donors, potential legacy donors, and people who have told you that they will be leaving a gift to your organization in their Will. Whether it's during a phone call, home visit, legacy giving workshop, donor appreciation event or fundraising event, the best way to promote insurance gifts are in one-on-one conversations with donors who can benefit from them (see the ideal insurance donor profile in *Chapter 6*). If you choose to mention it at an event or legacy giving workshop, invite your favourite insurance professionals to attend, to help answer questions.

You may feel it is intrusive to ask a lot of in-depth questions about your donor's giving strategies, to determine if someone who says he or she wants to give more is a good prospect for giving through insurance. You can ask this easy question to open the door to mentioning gifts of insurance:

"Your support is having such a profound impact on our work, and you've mentioned you'd like to do more. Do you have a plan in mind of how you'd like to make a significant meaningful gift? <If they mention a bequest through their Will> Would you mind telling me if you have already set aside the funds to fund this bequest? I ask this because I've seen other donors make some simple changes to the way they make their gift that has allowed them to give much more – without having to increase the size of their donation."

Funds already set aside can be used to purchase insurance products that can yield a guaranteed gift — and often a significantly larger gift — than cash delivered through a traditional bequest (see *Chapter 6*).

If you discover that a donor doesn't have a Will, doesn't want one, but wants to leave an estate gift by leaving instructions to have the residue from mutual funds/bonds/GICs/RRSPs, etc. given to your charity, you will want to explain that dying without a Will puts into motion a government process of asset disbursement, and that any informal instructions are not honoured (see *Chapter 5*).

Don't hand over your prospect lists to insurance professionals

If your charity has an established relationship with an insurance company or independent broker, resist the urge to hand over your prospect list and allow them to contact your donors directly by phone or through the mail. Although it may seem easier to get insurance professionals to do this work for you, they may find it difficult to explain simply how to marry insurance with philanthropy because this isn't part of advisors' official training. In addition, it can be seen as unethical for charities to have insurance salespeople cold-call their donors.

Network with insurance professionals and financial advisors

Some charities host breakfast or after-work meetings for advisors and bring in interesting guest speakers from within their charity who can give a first-person perspective on the organization's work and the impact it has. These kinds of meetings can keep your organization's work top of mind in advisors' minds during their conversations with their clients about their philanthropic goals.

You may wish to buy your favourite advisors a copy of *Ripple Effect: Growing your business with insurance and philanthropy*, the companion book to this one that educates professional advisors on how to best utilize insurance to help clients enhance their legacy giving.

Chapter 8

EFFECTIVELY
ADMINISTERING
YOUR CHARITY'S
INSURANCE GIFT PROGRAM

"How lovely to think that no one need
wait a moment; we can start now,
start slowly changing the world!"

— Anne Frank

I'm convinced that it would benefit our charity to promote giving through insurance. Now what?

Insurance gifts are relatively easy for a charity to administer.

The charity's only core duties are to monitor that donors who have made your charity the owner of a life insurance policy are paying their premiums on time, and remind donors who miss payments to pay them.

To fully reap all the benefits of running an effective insurance donation program, there is more to be done. Here is an outline of what has worked best for charities that are successfully managing insurance giving programs.

Evaluate if your organization has sufficient resources

Before you begin to actively promote receiving gifts of insurance, you should take a good look within your organization to see if you've got the infrastructure needed to run an insurance program.

Stewardship: Keep in mind that an insurance donor is like any bequest expectancy. You must continue to steward donors who have made your charity the owner and/or beneficiary of any insurance products. Insurance donors may be younger than the typical bequest donor, due to the fact that it can be less expensive for younger people to purchase policies. Do you have the ability to manage a 50-year relationship?

Staffing: Charities with large, thriving insurance programs swear that having planned giving staff oversee all the technicalities surrounding gifts of insurance — as opposed to getting Finance or Accounting staff to do so — is the key to their success. Planned giving staff better manage these relationships, and are much more sensitive at handling donors who may miss or stop paying premiums. After all, ceasing to pay premiums on a policy being donated to charity may stem from ill feelings about something the organization has done, hasn't done, or was perceived to have done. A caring conversation from a fundraiser may heal wounds that may otherwise be exacerbated by an accountant talking to donors using the language of debt collectors. Do you have staffing capacity in your development department to handle insurance giving?

These decisions will be easier to make by the time you reach the end of this chapter.

Developing a Gift Acceptance Policy

Before beginning to actively promote gifts of insurance, it is important to carefully think through what kinds of policies you are going to accept and how you are going to deal with potential donors.

Crafting these decisions into a Board-approved Gift Acceptance Policy helps to create a framework that current and future staff, executive volunteers, and your selected insurance advisors can work within. Here's a list of things to consider when crafting your policy:

What types of policies will our charity accept?

Despite the fact that each policy can be evaluated on its own unique attributes, you can make some of the more contentious decisions in advance:

- **Is there a minimum size of policy we will accept?** Consider that stewarding gifts of small policies of $5,000 - $10,000 or less — possibly for decades — may cost you more money than the final gift is worth.

- **Will we accept insurance policies that require our charity to pay premiums to keep it from lapsing?** Making this a "yes" or "no" decision may result in leaving significant funds on the table. Re-read the section on donations of this type of life insurance policy in *Chapter 4*. It outlines all the salient points to consider in carefully crafting your own answer.

- **Will we accept a policy in which our charity is a co-owner with the donor or another charity?** If you determine that the value or type of policy allows your charity to gain sufficient benefit from the policy's death benefit, accepting such a policy may be in your favour.[5]

What are the ideal types of insurance gifts that our charity would most prefer to receive?

Here is a list of the most secure, hassle-free insurance gifts that you should include in your Policy, and your favourite insurance advisors should be asked to promote. I recommend that you don't simply adopt this as an exclusive list, since you may receive future offers of other types of insurance gifts that may be of great benefit to your charity.

- Unneeded permanent life insurance policies that are fully-funded – their cash value will guarantee that the policy will never lapse.

- New permanent life insurance policies that will be paid off in less than 10 years, that generate a cash value to offset all future premiums. Examples of permanent insurance are whole life, T100 and universal life.

- New or existing policies that require payment for the balance in the donor's lifetime, and whose premiums are guaranteed to be paid by dedicated annuity payments (See Back-to-Back strategy, *Chapter 5*).

- Anyone can name your charity as the beneficiary on any kind of life insurance policy, annuity, or investments held in insurance companies, including segregated funds, guaranteed investment certificates, registered savings plans and

---

5 Canadian Revenue Agency Technical Interpretations 2009-031202 and 2011-0398461C6.

tax-free savings accounts. Often charities do not find out about these gifts while the donor is alive.

Under what circumstances will our charity decide to cash in a gifted policy?

Cashing in a policy and taking its cash surrender value will almost always result in a gift that is far less than a life insurance policy's death benefit. There are typically three reasons why charities decide to cash in policies:

- A young healthy person donates a policy that has premiums that must be paid for life. Whether they ask the charity to take on ownership and pay the premiums, or indicate they intend to do so themselves, this kind of policy is most likely to fail, unless the payments are backed up by an annuity generating payments dedicated to cover insurance premiums. (See the "Frank" example at the very beginning of this book).

- The charity develops urgent cash-flow problems.

- A smaller charity doesn't have the infrastructure in place to manage insurance policy gifts or donor stewardship for decades.

Deciding in advance what issues must be in place to cash in a policy will ensure that insurance gifts are managed to the charity's best advantage.

Can a donor restrict the use of funds from an insurance donation?

Being able to assign a specific use for a donation is attractive to many donors, but it may not be practical for smaller gifts. You may want to determine a minimum size of gift that allows a donor to designate their gift.

Who should pay for the actuarial evaluation needed to determine fair market value of an existing insurance policy?

When a donor wishes to donate a fully paid, self-funding whole life insurance policy that they no longer need (the most common kind of insurance gift), you can immediately give the donor a tax receipt for the cash surrender value. However, if the tax receipt is to be based on the fair market value (FMV), an actuary must be hired at a cost of about $2,000 to determine the FMV. Some charities ask the donor to cover this cost in a separate transaction, making a donation equal to the cost of the assessment, for which they get a charitable tax receipt. It is worth discussing in advance how your charity will handle gifts from donors who do not wish to cover the actuary's fee.

If your charity is named as the owner of a gifted policy, would you prefer that donors paying premiums send them to your charity or directly to the insurance company?

If you ask donors to send their premiums to you, it is easy to track their payments and know immediately if payments are missed. Yet this supplies your charity with extra monthly work by having to forward these premiums to the appropriate insurance companies. Keep in mind that direct debit arrangements can be made to automate this process, but it does turn your organization into a bill collector.

You can have your donors send their premiums directly to their insurance company. If they miss any payments, your charity, as the policy owner, will be notified. You should ensure that these notifications go to the planned giving department, who can sensitively do follow-up and learn why payments have stopped. At the end of the year, you can contact the insurance company and ask for a letter that confirms what payments have been made on the policies. You can use this confirmation to generate tax receipts to the donors.

Whether donors send your charity or the insurance company their premium payments, the donor is still eligible to receive tax receipts for the combined total of their annual payments.

Gift agreement

It is in your charity's best interest to have a gift agreement in place to clarify rules surrounding gifts of insurance, to help you track these donors, and to facilitate the execution of the legacy gift.

It is well worth the money to have a lawyer familiar with charity law draft a standard agreement to use with all insurance donors.

When meeting with the lawyer, you should discuss whether you should include points of this nature in your agreement:

- **Donor info:** Donor's full legal name, address, phone number(s), email address; name and contact information for second donor (for Joint-Last-to-Die Life Insurance Policies)
- **Donor ID:** Identification number assigned to the donor(s) by your fundraising software program
- **Type of gift:** Type of insurance product (e.g. life insurance policy; residual from annuity, insured GICs, RRSPs, RRIFs) being donated or being assigned to your charity as beneficiary
- **Insurer info:** Insurance company name; policy or product number; date on policy
- **Beneficiary info:** Whether your charity has been assigned as:
  - Owner and Beneficiary
  - Beneficiary only
  - Irrevocable Beneficiary

- Contingent Beneficiary
- Co-Beneficiary (charity is one of two or more beneficiaries)

Insurable interest: Normally, people buy life insurance for themselves. However, someone can purchase insurance based on the life of another, presuming the purchaser would suffer some kind of loss if the insured person died. This is called insurable interest. However, when a charity is named as the owner and beneficiary of a policy based on the life of a donor, the charity does not have an insurable interest on the donor. Your gift agreement must require the donor to formally register his or her consent to have a life insurance policy based on his or life, with your charity named as its owner and beneficiary.

Copy of policy: Checkbox to indicate that a copy of the policy is attached to the agreement

Preplanned funeral: If the donor has already chosen a funeral home and/or purchased a funeral plot, having this information can help you if you need to check if the donor has passed away.

Executor's contact information: Name, title and financial institution (if executor is a professional advisor), mailing address, telephone numbers, email address. Include checkbox that executor was given a form instructing them about the insurance gift and to inform insurance company of donor's death to activate the gift. (See *Appendix 3* for sample Executor form. You can also download a Word copy of the form at www.bequestinsurance.ca/Executor_Form.php)

For donations of new policies purchased expressly for making a charitable gift, include a pledge to pay premiums of $_____, and note the payment schedule desired by the donor (eg. monthly/annually/single payment that fully funds the policy). If policy is to be fully funded within a certain period of time, note how many years this will be, and when the last payment will be made.

For donations of pre-existing policies that the donor no longer needs:

- Section for donor agreement specifying that the charity will collapse permanent insurance policies and collect the cash surrender value. Include current cash surrender value and fair market value as evaluated by an actuary.

- Section for a donor who wishes for the charity to receive death benefit of a life insurance policy. Include a strongly worded pledge that the donor must sign to agree to continue making payments. Also note the dollar value of the regular premium payments and what the premium payment schedule is. In the case a donor has used a back-to-back strategy (purchasing an annuity to generate funds for premium payments), list the annuity, the type of annuity (life, term certain), insurance company and annuity number.

- Section for donating a whole life policy that is fully funded (cash surrender value is guaranteed to pay policy for life of insured). Include current cash surrender value and fair market value as evaluated by an actuary.

- Section for donating a universal life policy that is fully funded (cash surrender value is guaranteed to pay policy for life of insured). Include current cash surrender value and total value of premiums paid on policy.

- Section for donating a policy that will be fully funded in a fixed length of time. Include cost of premiums, payment schedule and the date policy will be fully funded.

Gift designation: Note any instructions the donor has on the use of funds received from insurance gift, or whether gift will be directed to area of greatest need. Also include contingency information on what will happen to these funds if the area of designation no longer exists or has dramatically changed by the time the gift is actually received. Include directions on whether gift is to be endowed, or dispensed over a period of time.

Conditions of acceptance could include the following points:

- Transfer of ownership of life insurance policy is conditional on the policy having the minimum face value/death benefit as decided upon by Board.

- That charity has the right to take out loans against the cash surrender value of a life insurance policy, or to use the cash value to fund urgent needs.

- If donor can no longer cover entire cost of premiums, that the charity will/will not pay the difference.

- What the charity may consider doing in the event of non-payment of premiums being paid by the donor, e.g.:

  - Use cash surrender value to continue to pay premiums

  - If cash surrender value is insufficient to pay premiums for estimated length of time until donor passes away, decrease the death benefit to the level that can be supported by existing cash value

  - Collapse the policy and claim the cash surrender value

  - Continue making payments on behalf of the donor

  - Find other donors who can continue to pay premiums

  - Buy an annuity for the purpose of paying premiums on policies that might otherwise lapse

  - Let policy lapse

- Official signatures: Donor(s) signature, printed name and date; Charity's representative – signature, printed name, title and date.

Donor stewardship

In the same way that you would maintain contact with a donor who has informed you of a gift in their Will, it is important to maintain a good relationship with those who have promised gifts of insurance. They, too, want to be kept up-to-date on the work of the organization, and feel your gratitude!

It is beneficial to mail them at least two communications pieces each year, whether it be donor newsletters accompanied by a personalized hand-written note, personalized letters, and/or birthday or holiday cards with handwritten notes. Keep an eye out for mail that is returned; it can either indicate the donor has moved or passed away.

Try phoning once a year to check in with the donor. If the number has changed, or no one picks up and there is no voicemail service, check www.canada411.ca or use the lettershop that does your direct mail to access the National Change of Address (NCOA) program and learn if the person has moved.

You can do an online search for their name and the word "obituary", or their name and the nearest funeral home to their last address (or the funeral home with which they pre-planned their funeral, noted on their gift agreement) to learn if they have died. You can also contact the donor's executor.

Claiming the death benefit from a donated policy

When the donor has passed away, if you have not received the policy's death benefit within a month, contact the executor and remind him or her that the donor pledged to make an insurance gift.

If the insurance policy or product has your charity named as _beneficiary_ (not owner), ask the executor to send a copy of the death certificate to the insurance company holding the donor's policy and to file an insurance claim.

If the donor has named your charity as _owner and beneficiary_, the executor must send a copy of the death certificate to your charity, and your organization is responsible for contacting the insurance company and filing an insurance claim. When this is done, the donor's charitable gift will usually be mailed to your charity within two to three weeks.

When a donor dies intestate, he or she will not have an executor. If you are aware that your charity has been named as beneficiary on any kind of insurance product or policy, and you learn that the donor has passed away, you must obtain a death certificate from the Ministry of the Attorney General and send it to the insurance company to claim your donation.

Tracking and receipting gifts of insurance

Tracking and appropriately receipting each insurance gift is a core responsibility of your charity.

You must track of all of your policies, donors and the premiums they pay. If your charity uses Raiser's Edge fundraising software, you can use the planned giving module to track policies and premium payments. Or you can create an Excel spreadsheet to track this information.

On the anniversary of each policy gifted to your charity or at the end of each calendar year, it is essential to ask the insurer for letter that indicates the amount of the premiums that have been paid over the past year, and note if payments have stopped. The letter will give you the information you need to issue accurate tax receipts to those paying the premiums on these policies.

Tax receipts may be issued whether the donor pays the premium directly to the insurance company, or contributes the premium amount to your charity which, in turn, pays the insurance company.[6]

Remember that you must not issue tax receipts on policies that name your charity as the beneficiary only. Because a

---

6 CRA's Interpretation Bulletin No. IT-244R3 – *Gifts by Individuals of Life Insurance Policies as Charitable Donation.*

beneficiary can be changed at any time, the only tax receipt a donor will receive is the one issued to his or her estate, for the amount your organization receives after the donor's death.

You can request in-force illustrations on policies to update you on the value of the death benefit at that time – depending on the type of policy, this amount may change as the donor ages. In addition, this document will reveal the amount of accumulated cash value, which may be relevant if your organization finds itself facing an urgent cash crisis that can only be solved by liquidating a policy for its cash surrender value, or taking out a loan by using the cash value as collateral.

Paying insurance premiums

Before you decide to take on premium payments for any insurance policies, it would be wise to get the help of an insurance professional to review the insurance contracts in question.

If your charity chooses to take on premium payments for a policy on which you have been named as an owner, it is critical to set up a system that ensures the premiums are paid on time. The most reliable is to set up an automatic direct debit payment to the insurance company.

Insurance companies offer a bit of leeway — usually 30 days after the premium due date — in which you can pay the premiums. If your payment occurs after the grace period, there can be very negative consequences:

- You may have to pay a penalty fee.
- The policy may lapse and become worthless.
- If the policy lapses, you may be able to reinstate it during a defined grace period that will be noted on in the fine print of your insurance policy contract (often two years). Doing so generally requires that you pay all premiums owing. The

insurance company may also require that the donor completes a short questionnaire on their current health situation, which may result in the premiums becoming more expensive.

- Make sure you take every possible precaution to ensure your policy doesn't lapse due to late premiums!

Have good professional advisors

Questions will arise surrounding gifts of insurance, and it is important to get to know trustworthy, unbiased insurance professionals who really understand integrating insurance into estate and legacy planning. Many charities seek an insurance professional to serve as a volunteer on a development committee or Foundation board.

Supply financial professionals with your gift acceptance policy so they know what kind of gifts you are willing to accept.

It is beneficial to have a list of good agents and brokers handy, in case a donor needs to ask an expert if integrating gifts of insurance suits their personal circumstances, and if so, how best to use it for tax and legacy planning.

There are two disadvantages to exclusively doing business with any one particular insurance company.

- Across the board, insurance products and rates can change frequently. The costs of premiums, the return on annuities, and the interest on insurance products often vary dramatically from company to company. Donors can usually get the best deal by using an independent insurance broker to shop the entire market for the product most appropriate for them, and then get the best price and rate of return available at that time.
- If your charity chooses to work exclusively with only one agent or broker, it will alienate other agents who won't go

out of their way to advise clients to give to your charity. It is best to work with a selection of insurance professionals, and keep them informed about the work of your charity through one-on-one meetings or annual breakfasts for financial advisors.

Promote gifts of insurance

Although it may not pay off to promote gifts of insurance using targeted direct mail, it is important to include information about it on your website, mention it as an option on direct mail reply forms, have a fact sheet ready for interested donors, and be willing to investigate the possibility in one-on-one conversations with people who are good potential candidates for giving in this way. See *Chapter 7* for detailed tips.

Chapter 9

FINAL THOUGHTS

"What is the use of living,
if not to strive for noble causes
and to make this muddled world
a better place for those who will live in it
after we are gone?"

— Winston Churchill

What in the world is left for you to say?!?

I hope that you've been inspired to think of using insurance for philanthropic purposes in new and powerful ways!

I strongly encourage Canadian fundraisers with legacy giving responsibilities to join the Canadian Association of Gift Planners (CAGP), and attend talks on insurance given at their periodic local meetings and the CAGP annual conference. Not only will you gain up-to-date information on using insurance in charitable giving, you will meet colleagues with experience in handling gifts of insurance, and financial professionals with specific expertise in integrating charitable giving in estate planning. The knowledge and contacts you will make will further deepen your knowledge of using insurance in charitable giving.

I must remind you that insurance giving strategies can vary from individual to individual. There are also a myriad of insurance products, and some products are created and eliminated periodically. When talking to donors about giving through insurance, advise them to consult with a trusted insurance professional who specializes in incorporating philanthropy into estate planning.

All information in this book is for information purposes only and should not be construed as legal or tax advice. Every effort has been made to ensure its accuracy, but errors and omissions are possible.

All comments related to taxation are general in nature and are based on 2015 Canadian tax legislation for Canadian residents, and are subject to change.

Examples in this book are current as of May 2015.

ADDITIONAL READING

Bronfman, Charles, & Jeffrey Solomon. (2009). *The Art of Giving – Where the Soul Meets a Business Plan*. Jossey-Bass.

"There are thousands of books that teach us how to make money, but very few that teach us how to give effectively," said Charles Bronfman. "Giving is easy, but giving effectively and strategically requires both self-awareness and a solid business sense. Together with my co-author, our aim is to help accelerate a new generation of philanthropists along what can be a very steep learning curve."

Green, Fraser, Beth McDonald, Jose van Herpt. (2007). *Iceberg Philanthropy - Unlocking Extraordinary Gifts from Ordinary Donors*. FLA Group.

Iceberg Philanthropy turns traditional planned giving on its head by showing fundraisers how very ordinary donors are making extraordinary gifts to charity in their Wills. With a powerful synergy of major gift strategy and direct market-ing tactics, *Iceberg Philanthropy* shows fundraisers how to extend their reach way beyond previous planned giving frontiers.

Minton, Frank & Lorna Somers. (1998) *Planned Giving for Canadians*. Somersmith.

Canada's planned giving bible – an excellent overall resource. A recently updated copy is available as a free ebook download to all Canadian Association of Gift Plan-ners members.

Pallota, Dan. (2008). *Uncharitable – How Restraints on Nonprofits Undermine their Potential*. Tufts University Press.

Most of your clients will want to evaluate whether they

should support a charity or not based on the cost of their administration expenses, how much the staff are paid, and how much is spent on fundraising. In a groundbreaking must-read book, Dan Pallotta argues that this Puritan ethic deprives nonprofits of tools and permissions freely used by the for-profit sector, which hobbles nonprofits from being able to effectively achieve their goals.

For a taste of what this book is about, listen to Dan Pallotta's TedTalk: http://bit.ly/1ooDyJI

Solie, David. (2004) *How to Say It to Seniors – Closing the Communications Gap with our Elders*. Penguin.

An invaluable tool for fundraisers who regularly have conversations with older donors, or anyone with older loved ones. Solie's meaningful insights, useful tools, and pragmatic advice will help you better communicate with seniors and better help them fulfill their needs and wishes. A must-read for every planned giving professional.

Turcotte, Martin. (2012) *Charitable Giving by Canadians*. Statistics Canada.

On average, 84% of Canadians 15 and older — or just under 24 million people — reported making at least one financial donation to a charitable or nonprofit organization. This number climbs to 94% if you include gifts of material goods or food. This Statistics Canada study released in 2012 details who constitutes a typical Canadian donor and what motivates them to give. http://bit.ly/1RgXQFe

APPENDICES

Appendix 1 — Canadian tax law surrounding donations of insurance

All legal guidelines can be read on the Canadian Revenue Agency's website in this Income Tax Interpretation Bulletin: http://bit.ly/1NhDuZ4

Government of Canada Income Tax Act on Registered Charity Disbursement Quotas in relation to unmatured gifts of insurance – Regulation 3702 (1) (vi) http://bit.ly/1NxKLs7

Appendix 2 — Change in the Ontario (Canada) Estate Administration Tax Act (effective January 1, 2013)

Changes made to the Ontario Estate Administration Tax Act (normally known as the "probate" process) can make it more difficult for charities to quickly receive bequests made through an individual's Will, making legacy gifts using insurance more advantageous to Canadian charities with Ontario donors.

The changes allow the Minister of Revenue to assess or reassess an estate for its tax payable for four years after the application for probate (officially known as the Certificate of Appointment of Estate Trustee) is made. With such an application, information must be submitted on an estate's assets, along with a payment of taxes owing. If the government suspects that an individual has undervalued assets to avoid paying the appropriate amount of tax, auditors may perform an inventory of all assets and will hold the executor responsible for any additional taxes owing.

If an executor wants to make sure that there are no challenges to the estate taxes, the executor may decide to wait four years before distributing assets, including distributing any charitable bequests.

Act respecting 2011 Budget measures, interim appropriations and other matters, Schedule 14 – Estate Administration Tax Act, 1998, Subsections 4.4 (Reassessments) & 4.5 (Time limit for assessment, reassessment). http://bit.ly/1HhVOo3

Appendix 3 — Sample document providing instructions on insurance donations to leave with Will for Executor

TO THE EXECUTOR OF <ENTER NAME>'S ESTATE

I, *<Enter full legal name>*, have left the following donation(s) of life insurance or insurance products to charity:

a. **Life insurance policy**, Policy number XXXXX, with *<Name of Insurance Company>*. On this policy, I have named *<legal name of charity>* as the owner and beneficiary / beneficiary / irrevocable beneficiary/co-beneficiary/ contingent beneficiary in the case that *<Name of primary beneficiary>* has predeceased me. Please contact the above noted insurance company and forward them a copy of my death certificate, to expedite my charity receiving the death benefit from this insurance policy. [To add if the charity has been named **owner** of the policy:] Please anticipate that the aforementioned charity will send to my estate a charitable tax receipt for the full value of the death benefit they will receive, which can be applied against 100% of my final year's net income. If the tax credit is larger than the taxes owing on the final return, the balance of the tax credit can be against 100% of my net income in the year before my death to reclaim taxes submitted in that year.

b. **Annuity <or Variable Annuity / Segregated Fund / GIC / RRSP / RRIF / any other insurance product held in an insurance company>**, Contract number XXXXX, with *<Name of Insurance Company>*. I have named *<legal name of charity>* as the <owner and beneficiary / beneficiary / irrevocable beneficiary/co-beneficiary/contingent beneficiary> of the aforementioned insurance product. The beneficiary should receive any residue remaining as of the date of my death. Please contact the above noted insurance company and if there are any residual funds left, forward the insurance company a copy of my death certificate.

Anticipate that the aforementioned charity will send to my estate a charitable tax receipt for any residual funds that it will receive, which should be applied against 100% of my final year's net income. If the tax credit is larger than the taxes owing on the final return, the balance of the tax credit should be used against 100% of my net income in the year before my death to reclaim taxes submitted in that year.

1. Statements and other documentation of this life insurance policy / insurance products can be found in *<location of insurance paperwork>*.

2. I have made the charity aware that they will be receiving this gift.
   or
   I have not made the charity aware that they will be receiving this gift.

3. I have made my family / loved ones aware of this gift.
   or
   I have purposely not shared information about this gift with my family, loved ones or friends. I wish to keep this gift private. Please do not let them know I have made this gift.
   or
   During my lifetime, I have purposely not shared information about this gift with my family, loved ones or friends. After my death, and after my charity has received the gift (*after one month of the insurance company receiving my death certificate from you*), please share information about this donation with *<Names of specific individuals>*.

Signature: _____

Date: _____

Printed name of Signer: _____

To download a Word version of this form, go to www.bequestinsurance. ca/Executor_Form.php

Appendix 4 — Fundraiser's Cheat Sheet to Using Insurance Products for Charitable Giving

Fundraiser's Cheat Sheet to Using Insurance Products for Charitable Giving	
Insurance product /ownership &/or beneficiary designation	**Fully Funded Life Insurance Policy** Charity is named owner & beneficiary **pg. 43**
Ideal qualities to make best charitable gif	• **Fully paid-up policies that grow in value over lifetime of donor** with sufficient accumulated cash value to keep policy in force until death of purchaser • **Policies donated with cash or securities** to pay all premiums for life • **Policies with payments covered by automated annuity payments** (Back-to-Back arrangement) • **Single-pay policies** that have been fully funded with one payment
Risk	• None
Benefits to donors and/or their estates	• Donor receives immediate charitable receipt for policy's cash value or fair market value (as determined by an actuary) • Tax receipts can be used to lower taxes in year of gift, or in any of five ensuing years to lower taxes • No benefit to estate/no tax receipt for gifted death benefit • Normally incontestable
Benefits to charitable organization	• Immediate access to cash value • Guaranteed tax-free death benefit, received within 2-3 weeks of insurance company receiving proper paperwork from executor • Death benefit could grow in value over lifetime of donor • Normally incontestible

Fundraiser's Cheat Sheet to Using Insurance Products for Charitable Giving	
Insurance product /ownership &/or beneficiary designation	**Short-Pay Life Insurance Policy** Charity is named owner & beneficiary **pg. 34**
Ideal qualities to make best charitable gift	• Policies that become fully funded by the donor over a defined period of time (ideally 10 years or less) and that grow in value over lifetime of donor
Risk	• Short pay policies have lower risk of lapsing
Benefits to donors and/or their estates	• Simple and very affordable way to pay a little and give significantly more • Donor receives annual tax receipts for premium payments, which lower real cost of premiums by 40-50% • Tax receipts can be used by donor in year of gift, or in any of 5 ensuing years to lower taxes • Normally incontestable
Benefits to charitable organization	• Short time frame on fully funding the policy reduces risk of policy lapsing • Immediate access to cash value • Guaranteed tax-free death benefit, received within 2-3 weeks of insurance company receiving proper paperwork from executor • Death benefit grows in value over lifetime of donor • Normally incontestible

Fundraiser's Cheat Sheet to Using Insurance Products for Charitable Giving	
Insurance product /ownership &/or beneficiary designation	**Pay-for-Life or T100 (term insurance paid to age 100) Life Insurance Policy** Charity is named owner & beneficiary **pg. 52**
Ideal qualities to make best charitable gift	• Look for policies that grow in value over time, and whose premium payments are guaranteed by Back-to-Back arrangement (donor purchases an annuity whose payments are automatically used to pay insurance premiums)
Risk	• Higher risk of lapsing due to donor stopping payment of insurance premiums
Benefits to donors and/or their estates	• Donor receives annual tax receipts for premium payments, which lower real cost of premiums by 40-50% • Tax receipts can be used by donor in year of gift, or in any of 5 ensuing years to lower taxes • Normally incontestable
Benefits to charitable organization	• Immediate access to cash value • Guaranteed tax-free death benefit, received within 2-3 weeks of insurance company receiving proper paperwork from executor • Death benefit could grow in value over lifetime of donor • Normally incontestible

Fundraiser's Cheat Sheet to Using Insurance Products for Charitable Giving	
Insurance product /ownership &/or beneficiary designation	**Life Insurance Policy (Any type)** Donor retains ownership & charity is named as beneficiary **pg. 50**
Ideal qualities to make best charitable gift	• Ideal for donors who can benefit from tax relief for their estate (payment of taxes, probate fees and capital gains tax), after their death *This kind of policy is most likely to come as a surprise to charity*
Risk	• Donor may change mind and change beneficiary at any time
Benefits to donors and/or their estates	• Donor's estate receives charitable receipt for full value of death benefit as of the date of transfer to the charity • Receipt can offset taxes from year of death, year before, or as of 2016 on taxes owed by the estate up to 3 years after death • Gift is often significantly larger than premiums paid on policy • Donor can change beneficiary if a family need arises or if their charitable giving priorities change • Normally incontestable
Benefits to charitable organization	• Receive full value of policy within 2-3 weeks of executor officially informing insurance company of the donor's death • Normally incontestable

Fundraiser's Cheat Sheet to Using Insurance Products for Charitable Giving	
Insurance product /ownership &/or beneficiary designation	Life Annuity (Donation of any residual value) Charity is named as beneficiary **pg. 57**
Ideal qualities to make best charitable gift	• Popular insurance product commonly used by retirees to provide tax-smart guaranteed income for life. For donors without children (or whose children are well-off), it is quick and easy for donor to assign a charity to beneficiary of any residual value
Risk	• None • If donor lives long enough, annuity may have no residual value
Benefits to donors and/or their estates	• Changing current beneficiary to charitable beneficiary is fast and easy • Donor's estate receives charitable receipt for full value of death benefit as of the date of transfer to the charity • Receipt can offset taxes from year of death, year before, or as of 2016 on taxes owed by the estate up to 3 years after death • Gift is often significantly larger than premiums paid on policy • Donor can change beneficiary if a family need arises or if their charitable giving priorities change • Normally incontestable
Benefits to charitable organization	• If donor dies before the initial lump-sum invested in annuity is exhausted, residual value may be substantial • Receive annuity's residual value within 2-3 weeks of the insurance company receiving proper paperwork from executor • Normally incontestable

Fundraiser's Cheat Sheet to Using Insurance Products for Charitable Giving	
Insurance product /ownership &/or beneficiary designation	**Life Annuity (Donation of annuity)** Charity is named as owner & beneficiary **pg. 57**
Ideal qualities to make best charitable gift	• Great for charities who can benefit from guaranteed annual payments spread out over lifetime of donor, and a possible gift of residual funds if donor passes away before initial investment in annuity is completely exhausted • Advise donor to use insurance broker to shop for annuities; look for product that offers largest payments
Risk	• None
Benefits to donors and/or their estates	• Donor can turn lump-sum cash gift into annuity and annuity will meter out annual gifts to charity over donor's lifetime; residual goes to charity upon donor's death • Immediate tax receipt for lump-sum used to purchase annuity; no additional receipt to estate if total value charity receives is larger than initial lump sum • Tax receipts can be used by donor in year of gift, or in any of 5 ensuing years to lower taxes
Benefits to charitable organization	• Gift that begins to deliver benefits right away • Provides reliable, guaranteed income over lifetime of donor; income can be delivered monthly, quarterly, or annually • If donor lives long enough, charity may receive more than the lump sum used to initially purchase the annuity • Normally incontestable

Fundraiser's Cheat Sheet to Using Insurance Products for Charitable Giving	
Insurance product /ownership &/or beneficiary designation	**Term Certain Annuity** Charity is named as owner & beneficiary **pg. 39**
Ideal qualities to make best charitable gift	• Charity will receive guaranteed annual payments spread out over the fixed term of annuity, and a possible gift of residual funds if donor passes away before the end of the term • Advise donor to use insurance broker to shop for annuities; look for product that offers largest payments
Risk	• None • Charity must pay tax on interest portion of payment (a small % of each payment)
Benefits to donors and/or their estates	• Immediate donation receipt for fair market value (as determined by actuary) • Tax receipts can be used by donor in year of gift, or in any of 5 ensuing years to lower taxes
Benefits to charitable organization	• Gift that begins to deliver benefits right away • Provides reliable, guaranteed income over term of annuity; income can be delivered monthly, quarterly, or annually • Charity receives balance of funds left in annuity if donor passes away before end of annuity's term • Normally incontestable

Fundraiser's Cheat Sheet to Using Insurance Products for Charitable Giving	
Insurance product /ownership &/or beneficiary designation	**Variable Annuities** Charity is named as beneficiary **pg. 142**
Ideal qualities to make best charitable gift	• Great for charities who can benefit from guaranteed annual payments spread out over lifetime of donor, and a possible gift of residual funds if donor passes away before initial investment in annuity is completely exhausted • Advise donor to use insurance broker to shop for annuities; look for product that offers largest payments
Risk	• Donor may change mind and change beneficiary at any time
Benefits to donors and/or their estates	• Donation of residue helps reduce estate taxes
Benefits to charitable organization	• Popular insurance product commonly used to by retirees to provide guaranteed income for life. If donor dies before average age of death, residual value may be substantial • Receive remaining value within 2-3 weeks of executor officially informing insurance company of the donor's death

Fundraiser's Cheat Sheet to Using Insurance Products for Charitable Giving	
Insurance product /ownership &/or beneficiary designation	**Charitable Gift Annuity** Purchased through charity, making charity owner and beneficiary **pg. 58**
Ideal qualities to make best charitable gift	• To offer donor largest possible annuity payments for life, charity should shop around for insurance company that offers largest possible annuity payments at the time of purchase
Risk	• None
Benefits to donors and/or their estates	• Donor benefits from tax-smart guaranteed income for life that is usually much higher than other guaranteed income streams • Income received on annuity will reduce the risk of claw-back on income-tested government pensions (eg. OAS) • Donor makes generous donation and gets immediate tax receipt to reduce current taxes, or taxes in ensuing 5 years • Possible tax receipt to donor's estate if annuity has residual value when donor dies
Benefits to charitable organization	• Large immediate donation received • If donor dies when there is still residual value in their annuity, charity receives residual funds

Fundraiser's Cheat Sheet to Using Insurance Products for Charitable Giving	
Insurance product /ownership &/or beneficiary designation	**Insured GICs** Charity is named as beneficiary **pg. 67**
Ideal qualities to make best charitable gift	• Rates of return can vary from insurance company to insurance company. It is best to use an insurance broker to get the best rate of return
Risk	• Donor may change mind and change beneficiary at any time
Benefits to donors and/or their estates	• Tax receipt to estate for full value as of the date of transfer to the charity, which can offset estate & probate taxes, and capital gains taxes • Receipt can offset taxes from year of death, year before, or as of 2016 on taxes owed by the estate up to 3 years after death • Donor can change beneficiary if a family need arises or if their charitable giving priorities change • Normally incontestable
Benefits to charitable organization	• Receive value of GIC within 2-3 weeks of executor officially informing insurance company of the donor's death • Normally incontestable

Fundraiser's Cheat Sheet to Using Insurance Products for Charitable Giving	
Insurance product /ownership &/or beneficiary designation	**Segregated Funds** Charity is named as beneficiary **pg. 67**
Ideal qualities to make best charitable gift	• Rates of return can vary from insurance company to insurance company. It is best to use an insurance broker to get the best rate of return
Risk	• Donor may change mind and change beneficiary at any time
Benefits to donors and/or their estates	• Tax receipt to estate for full value as of the date of transfer to the charity, which can offset estate & probate taxes, and capital gains taxes • Receipt can offset taxes from year of death, year before, or as of 2016 on taxes owed by the estate up to 3 years after death • Donor can change beneficiary if a family need arises or if their charitable giving priorities change • Normally incontestable
Benefits to charitable organization	• Receive value of fund within 2-3 weeks of executor officially informing insurance company of the donor's death • Normally incontestable

Please note that risks of accepting any gifts of insurance are greatly diminished when you know the donor, and the primary intention of their gift is to be charitable, and not to solely make a donation for tax relief.

GLOSSARY

Not all of these words or concepts are used in this book, but may take some of the mystery out of conversations you will have with financial advisors, lawyers or accountants.

Accumulation annuity
See guaranteed interest account.

Actuary
A business professional qualified to mathematically calculate commercial and financial risks and probabilities on uncertain future events, based on statistics and laws of averages. Actuaries are used by insurance companies to calculate insurance premiums, and by charities to determine the fair market value of life insurance policies, for tax receipting purposes.

Adjustable life insurance
A permanent life insurance policy whose premiums get less expensive when interest rates rise, and more expensive when interest rates drop.

Agent
See insurance agent.

Annual renewal term insurance
See year renewal term insurance.

Annuitant

1. A person who receives the benefits of an annuity or pension. An annuity contract can have more than one annuitant.

2. A person upon whom a life insurance contract is based.

Annuity
A series of income payments or receipts made at yearly or at

other regular intervals for life or specific period of time or term.

Annuity contract
A contractual agreement with a life insurance company that will provide regular payments for life or at regular intervals in exchange for a lump sum payment. The owner of the annuity contract may or may not be the annuitant.

Assuris
A not-for-profit organization that protects Canadian insurance policyholders if their life insurance company fails. It minimizes the loss of benefits and ensures a quick transfer of policies to a solvent company, where their protected benefits will continue. Assuris guarantees policyholders will retain 100% of the values up to certain maximum thresholds and after that at least 85% of the insurance benefits they are promised, including death, health expense, monthly income and cash value. For deposit-type products like *guaranteed investment certificates*, Assuris guarantees the owner will retain 100% of their accumulated value up only to $100,000, just like the Canada Deposit Insurance Corporation coverage found in banks and trust companies.

Back-to-back strategy
Also known as insured annuities. When an individual guar-antees that a gifted insurance policy with life-long premium payments does not lapse by purchasing an annuity whose life-long payments are used to pay their insurance premiums.

Beneficiary
The individual or organization that receives life insurance proceeds or the residue remaining in insured investment products upon the death of the insured. All insurance products and investments allow the owner to assign a beneficiary to receive the policy's death benefit, or any residual amount left in annuities or other investments on the insured/owner's death.

Multiple beneficiaries are allowed. They can include individuals, businesses/organizations and charities.

Cash value/Cash surrender value
The cash an insurance company will pay to the insurance policy owner if his or her policy is voluntarily terminated before its maturity or before the death of the person insured. This cash value is the savings component of most permanent (not term) life insurance policies. When cashing out a policy, the insurance company first deducts any withdrawn interest and loans taken out by the owner against the policy to determine its current net cash value.

Certificate of deposit
See guaranteed investment certificate.

Charitable gift annuities
Also known as gift plus annuities or reinsured charitable gift annuities. A donation strategy offered to donors directly by certain charities. Popular with retirees who want to receive regular, guaranteed income for life, while also making a significant charitable gift. The donor makes an upfront payment for their annuity to the charity, which retains a minimum of 20 percent as a charitable gift, which is receipted immediately. The charity then funds an annuity with the balance of the funds, and directs the annuity payments to the donor.

Co-beneficiary
When a person assigns more than one beneficiary to their insurance policies, annuities or insurance investment products, beneficiaries are referred to as co-beneficiaries.

Community foundation
Non-profit organizations that help Canadians invest in building strong and resilient places to live, work and play. They can be employed to help facilitate charitable gifts. In Canada, community foundations can be identified through Community

Foundations of Canada (http://communityfoundations.ca/).

Commuted value
The present value of the future payments at a point in time of an annuity.

Commuting
Converting an annuity to its equivalent lump sum value.

Contingent beneficiary
Any insurance product can be assigned one or more back-up or contingent beneficiaries – people or organizations who will receive funds from insurance products if the primary beneficiary(ies) predecease the insured, or in the case of an charitable beneficiary, the charity ceases to exist before the death of the donor.

Contract
Term used by insurance agents/brokers to describe any insurance product purchased by a client.

Death benefit
The amount payable to a beneficiary(ies) of a life insurance policy or insurance product such as a GIC, segregated fund or annuity, after the insured person has died. If there is more than one beneficiary, each beneficiary gets whatever portion of the death benefit that was specified by the owner of the insurance contract. Beneficiaries cannot be changed by anyone other than the contract owner, not even by the owner's power of attorney. Death benefits can be a fixed (*or level*) amount as defined in the insurance contract, or can increase or decrease over time.

Deferred annuity
A term or life annuity contract in which the payments do not commence until a specific date that may be based upon the annuitant's age. The premium for the deferred annuity can be funded with a lump sum or through periodic payments.

Dependent
A person who relies on another for support or their primary source of income. Examples can include spouse, minor child, infirm child over 18.

Disbursement quota
The minimum legally defined amount a Canadian registered charity is obliged to spend each year on its charitable activities or on gifts to qualified donees (e.g. other registered charities). The disbursement quota (DQ) is based on the value of the charity's property not used for charitable activities or administration. Income received from gifts of life insurance is not considered fundraised income, and is not considered when calculating the DQ. Also, *unmatured life insurance policies* are not considered a charitable asset and are not counted when calculating the DQ.

Face amount / Face value
The amount of insurance coverage purchased by the policyholder.

Fair market value
A complicated calculation done by an actuary on a life insurance policy to determine its value at the time of the evaluation, following guidelines in the Canadian Revenue Agency's Information Circular IC-89-3. This amount is often larger than a policy's cash surrender value and less than its death benefit. The fee for an actuary to perform a fair market value on a policy can be in the $2,000 range.

Fixed annuity
An insurance contract in which the insurance company contractually guarantees payments to the annuitant for the term of the contract in exchange for a lump sum.

Fully-funded policy
Also known as a paid-up policy. A life insurance policy that has

accumulated sufficient cash value to cover the cost of all future premiums, without further payments from the insured.

Gift plus annuities
See charitable gift annuities.

Graded premiums
Policies with premiums that increase incrementally for a certain number of years, and thereafter remain level. Attractive to younger people who anticipate growth in future earnings.

Guaranteed interest account (GIA)
Also known as a guaranteed investment account or an accumulation annuity. Valued as a low-risk investment, the GIA is a deposit-type investment product offered by insurance companies, similar to GICs found at banks. Deposits into GIAs are accumulated for the purpose of providing a guaranteed lump sum in the future. When a GIA matures, the owner has the option of rolling the lump sum (principal plus accrued interest) into an annuity, or receiving the cash surrender value. GIAs offer holding periods of one to five years or more at guaranteed interest rates. Additional benefits include the residual value passing to named beneficiary(ies) outside of the estate to ease the transfer of wealth, possible creditor protection, and a guaranteed death benefit that includes the principal and all accrued interest.

Guaranteed investment certificate
Also known as GICs, certificate of deposit, time deposit or term deposit. Investment vehicles, sold by banks, trust companies and credit unions, which offer a guaranteed rate of return over a 1 to 5 year period. Valued as a low-risk investment.

Guaranteed minimum withdrawal benefit (GMWB)
An annuity with contractually guaranteed minimum payments for life or a given period. Payments may rise over time, depending on the performance of underlying investments.

Guaranteed premium return annuity
A *life annuity* that includes a guarantee that at least the full amount of the initial investment or premium payment will be paid out.

Immediate annuity
Usually refers to an annuity whose first payment is one month after the annuity is purchased, although by strict definition the first payment could take place within one year of purchase.

Increasing term insurance
See year renewal term insurance.

Indexed annuity
An annuity that includes a provision for increased payments over time, normally as a hedge against inflation.

In-force
An adjective used by insurance professionals that describes an active insurance policy.

In-force illustration
Details supplied by an insurance company on the current and future status and value of a life insurance policy as it stands at that time. The illustration includes the face value of the policy, cost of premium payments, accumulated cash value, the change in size of the policy over time (if any), and the death benefit. It will also indicate if the policy will lapse, and how much needs to be added to keep the policy from lapsing. Also, an in-force illustration can be requested to project certain assumptions for the future on an existing policy – for example, what would happen to a policy's death benefit if the policy's premiums are increased or decreased by a certain amount.

Insurability
The conditions on a life insurance applicant that are required by the life insurance company. To determine whether to issue a policy and the amount of premium to charge, an insurance

company conducts an underwriting process that takes into consideration such things as the health and financial situation of the insured, their age, whether they smoke or not, their weight and occupation, and the amount of life insurance already in force on the life of that person.

Insurance agent
Insurance agents help clients choose insurance policies that suit their needs. Clients include individuals, families and businesses. Captive agents work for and only sell a single insurance company's products or specified products of other insurance companies. Independent insurance agents (*or brokers*), represent several companies. Agents must usually be licensed within the province or territory in which they do business.

Insurable interest
To prevent mischief and/or speculation on the death of persons unconnected to a life insurance policy buyer, a life insurance policy can be purchased only by those who would suffer some kind of loss if the insured dies. They are said to have an "insurable interest." In the case of a charity owning a policy based on the life of a donor, the charity does not have an insurable interest on the donor, but all that is required to validate the donation of a life insurance policy is the donor's written consent noted on the beneficiary section of an insurance application or on a beneficiary change form – a minor formality.

Insurance broker
An insurance broker (also insurance agent) qualified to sell, solicit and negotiate insurance in the province or territory in which they are licensed. Canadian brokers must be licensed by each province or territory in which they do business.

Insured (The)
Also see *insurable interest*. The individual on whose life an insurance policy is based. Policy proceeds are paid upon the

death of the insured. The owner and the insured are often the same person, but they need not be the same.

Insured annuities
See back-to-back strategy.

Insurer
Insurance company that issues the insurance policy.

Irrevocable beneficiary
When the beneficiary status of a life insurance policy, annuity or any other insurance product is made irrevocable, it can only be changed with the permission of the named beneficiary. The irrevocable beneficiary also has to agree to adding other beneficiaries, or to surrendering (or collapsing) the policy before the death of the owner for the purpose of collecting the cash surrender value. However, the policy owner can still let such a policy lapse by not paying premiums, unless ordered by the court to continue paying the premiums.

Joint and last survivor annuity
A pension that is payable to two annuitants, and that includes a provision that payments continue for the life of the survivor after the first annuitant dies.

Joint last-to-die life insurance policy
Life insurance policies based on insuring two lives (a couple, siblings or close friends). The policy remains in force when the first of the two insured persons die; the death benefit only goes to the beneficiary after the death of the second insured person.

Level cost of insurance
Life insurance premiums that remain the same over the life of an insurance contract.

Life annuity
An annuity where payments are guaranteed for the life of the annuitant(s).

Life annuity with a guaranteed term
A life annuity that includes a clause that guarantees that payments will continue for a specific period, even if the annuitant dies before the guaranteed period expires. If the annuitant dies before the term, the guaranteed payments can be continued to beneficiaries as 'successor annuitants' for the duration of the contract or beneficiaries may receive a lump sum.

Life income fund (LIF)
A registered retirement income fund into which funds previously held in pension funds have been transferred. There are annual minimum and maximum amounts that can be withdrawn from the plan, as specified by the Income Tax Act. A LIF can be converted to a life annuity.

Life pay insurance
For more, see T-100 life insurance. Life insurance policies that require premiums to be paid until the insured dies.

Limited pay life insurance
See short-pay life insurance.

Locked-in retirement account (LIRA)
Also known as a locked-in retirement income fund (LRIF) in British Columbia, Nova Scotia, PEI, Yukon, NW Territories and by the Federal government. A registered retirement savings plan into which funds previously held in pension funds have been transferred and are held until the legal age of retirement, when the owner is required to begin extracting income. At that point the LIRA or LRIF is converted to a life income fund (LIF).

Locked-in retirement income fund (LRIF)
Also known as a locked-in RRIF. A retirement fund that receives funds from a locked-in retirement account and provides retirement income by that is limited by minimum and maximum withdrawal amounts.

Locked-in RRIF (LRIF)
See locked-in retirement income fund.

Locked-in RRSP (LRSP)
See locked-in retirement account.

Medical examination
Part of the insurance underwriting process, to determine whether an individual is insurable. Depending on the type and size of insurance policy, an applicant may have to either answer a written questionnaire about their health, have blood or urine taken by a nurse sent from a company that specifically completes medical examinations for insurance companies, or may require a more thorough exam or documentation from the applicant's family doctor.

Minimum amount
The amount that must be withdrawn from a RRIF each year, beginning the year after the RRIF is established, in accordance with the Income Tax Act – ITA 146.3(1).

Modified premium life insurance
Policies with premiums that remain fixed at a relatively low level for a certain number of years, then increase substantially in a single year to the level where they remain. Attractive option for younger people who anticipate growth in future earnings.

Net present value calculation
Also known as net present worth. A mathematical calculation to estimate the current value of an insurance policy (or other financial investments).

Normal annuity
An annuity that for income tax purposes calculate the interest and principal according to an amortization schedule, whereby early payments consist of a higher proportion of interest than later payments.

Old Age Security Program (OAS)
A monthly payment available to most Canadians 65 years of age and older who meet the Canadian legal status and residence requirements. Source: Old Age Security Pension, Service Canada. http://bit.ly/1GGGGRc

Owner
The individual or entity that owns a life insurance policy (also known as "the insurance contract"). The owner is usually the insured, and is responsible for paying premiums. In the case of policies purchased by donors who have assigned charities to be their owners, the donor who is insured is responsible for making the premium payments. If the donor has to stop making payments, the charity can continue making the payments, or collapse the policy and extract whatever net cash value has been accumulated.

Paid-up policy
See fully-funded policy.

Participating life insurance policies
Typically, these are life insurance contracts with a growing death benefit such as a whole life participating policies. Premiums paid on the policies are invested, which creates a growing cash value that is annually added to the policy as a dividend. The dividend can be relatively generous but is usually not contractually guaranteed. The dividend can be used different ways by the policy holder; e.g. to pay the insurance policy's premium payment or withdrawn for immediate use. Or, the dividend can be kept within the insurance contract as a deposit to generate interest much like a savings account at a bank.

Permanent life insurance
Life insurance policies where a death benefit is guaranteed when the insured passes away (provided the policy is in-force). T-100, whole life and universal life policies are examples of permanent insurance.

Policy

A legal contract between an individual or company and an insurance company (the insurer). Policies specify what risks are covered by the insurer; under what circumstances the insurer will pay the policy beneficiaries; how much money or type of benefit the insured will receive upon death or if the insured makes a claim; and who will be the beneficiary(ies) of the policy.

Premium offset

The cash value of a policy which pays the premiums (cost of insurance) until the cash value is completely depleted. In some cases, policies can accumulate enough cash value to pay the cost of insurance for the remainder of the insured's life.

Premiums

Payments made on life insurance policies.

Prescribed annuity

Provides payments that have a level interest component throughout the life of the contract. Available only for non-registered plans are very attractive for those seeking higher income through lower income taxes.

Probate

The legal procedure to validate a Will, formally confirm the appointment of the executor, and pay estate taxes. Officially known in Ontario as "Certificate of Appointment of Estate Trustee With a Will" or "Certificate of Appointment of Estate Trustee Without a Will". Probate taxes and related fees vary depending on where in Canada the deceased lived, and the value of his or her estate's assets. Typically a lawyer is employed to file and process a probate application on behalf of the executor. There may also be accountant's fees to prepare the application. These additional fees may be for time spent on an hourly basis, or on a percentage of the size of the estate, or both.

Quick pay life insurance policies
See short-pay life insurance.

Registered annuity
An annuity purchased from an insurance company with transferred registered savings, like Registered Retirement Savings Plans (RRSPs), Locked-in Retirement Account funds (LIRA) or Registered Retirement Income Funds (RRIFs).

Registered funds
Also known as tax-deferred savings. Savings held within registered plans. These include: Registered Retirement Savings Plans (RRSPs), Registered Retirement Income Funds (RRIFs), Locked-in Retirement Account funds (LRIFs), and Locked-in Retirement Accounts (LIRAs). When these are donated to charity, their entire value goes to the charity; the charitable tax receipt received will help to offset the income taxes owing on these accounts. In Ontario, Canada, probate taxes on registered accounts are waived if the entire residual amount is donated to a registered charity and/or other named beneficiaries.

Registered Retirement Income Fund (RRIF)
A Registered Retirement Income Fund (RRIF) is a tax-deferred retirement plan under Canadian tax law. Individuals use an RRIF to generate income from the savings accumulated under their Registered Retirement Savings Plan (RRSP). As with an RRSP, an RRIF account is registered with the Canada Revenue Agency. Individuals must convert an RRSP/LIRA to an income product, such as a RRIF, LRIF, or an annuity by December 31st in the year they turn 71. Income received from a RRIF is taxed at the highest rate as regular income.

Registered Retirement Savings Plan (RRSP)
A legal trust registered with the Canada Revenue Agency that is used by individuals to save for retirement. RRSP contributions are tax deductible and funds in RRSP accounts are deferred until the money is withdrawn. Money withdrawn

from a RRSP is tax deferred until the money is withdrawn.

Reinsured charitable gift annuities
See charitable gift annuities.

Segregated funds
Investment funds offered by insurance companies. They combine characteristics of the income and growth potential of a mutual fund. They add the security of capital guarantees, and many of the tax and estate benefits of a life insurance policy Segregated funds are invested in a managed pool of selected stocks, bonds, debentures and even other funds. Many estates can benefit from tax relief and increased income to heirs if charities are named as beneficiaries of these funds.

Short-pay policies
Also known as quick-pay or limited pay policies. Life insurance policies that can be fully funded and self-sustaining within a pre-determined period of time, or with a single payment.

Single life annuity
An annuity where payments are guaranteed for the life of a single annuitant.

Single pay life insurance policy
A policy that can be fully funded with one payment.

Specified death benefit
A predetermined fixed value to be received by beneficiaries of a life insurance policy.

Split-value life insurance policy
Also known as co-beneficiaries. When there are two or more beneficiaries assigned to a life insurance policy.

Spousal Registered Retirement Income Fund
Any RRIF created from a spousal or common-law Registered Retirement Savings Plan.

Spousal (or common-law) Registered Retirement Savings Plan
Intended as an effective way for couples to split taxable income
at retirement. An RRSP funded by a person (usually the higher
income earning spouse), up to their own annual RRSP limit,
for the benefit of their spouse or common-law partner to
receive income. The contributing spouse claims the annual tax
deductions on the contributions they make into the spousal
RRSP.

Straight-life annuity
An insurance contract that provides nothing more than
periodic payments to an annuitant until his or her death.

Successor annuitant
An option offered by most insurance contracts. A successor
annuitant receives continued payments after the death of the
original annuitant. For example, an owner and annuitant of a
RRIF may elect to have RRIF payments continue to go to his
spouse or common-law partner after his death.

T-100 life insurance
Permanent insurance policies that require a policy holder to
pay either monthly or annual premiums for the rest of his or
her life, or to age 100, whichever comes first. These policies do
not offer the owner the option of making additional payments
above the cost of insurance to produce a cash value that will
pay future premium payments. It would be extremely rare that
a T-100 would have a cash value.

Term certain annuity
A contract for the annuitant to receive regular and periodic
payments for a specified period of time or term. Includes a
guarantee that the payments will be made for the full term,
even if the annuitant dies before the term expires.

Term deposit
See guaranteed investment certificate.

Term insurance

Insurance provided for a specific time period and which pays a death benefit if the insured dies within that period. Often, no cash value accumulates in these policies. The death benefit may not change while the policy is in force, or benefits may decrease in tandem with a decreased obligation insured by the policy. Often used as a cheap substitute for mortgage insurance. If the policy owner does not die during the policy's term, the policy is collapsed and becomes valueless, with the exception of Term 100 insurance, which is a form of permanent insurance. Most insurance companies allow term insurance to be converted into a permanent insurance policy, which may become a charitable gift opportunity.

Underwriting

Insurance companies study the risk they take on by insuring life insurance applicants through an underwriting process. Underwriters look at such things as how much in-force insurance applicants own, and calculate risk based on applicants' health, weight, gender, age, whether they smoke, and sometimes their occupation. After completion of a medical history questionnaire and/or a simple or more complex medical examination, underwriters decide how much coverage an individual can receive, what the insurance premium payments will be, or whether applicants are too high risk and therefore uninsurable. By measuring these risks, underwriters work to protect the long-term viability of their insurance company, and its ability to meet all its obligations to its clients.

Universal life insurance

Universal life policies are a type of permanent insurance in which the premiums are invested and generate a growing tax-free cash value. These are often ideal for donors who want to make a donation of an insurance policy that becomes fully funded and self-sustaining. Over the payment period (which can be as little as one payment or can be set for a certain number of years or life), universal policies can accumulate sufficient cash value to pay all future premiums. As charitable donations, policies that are expected to be guaranteed to be self-funding, and that also guarantee a minimum death benefit are usually the best fit. This product can be used for *short-pay policies*.

Unmatured life insurance policies
Life insurance policies that are still in effect either because the person on whose life the policy is insured is still alive, or the term on the policy has not yet expired.

Unregistered annuity
An annuity purchased with unregistered funds.

Variable annuity
An insurance investment product often used for retirement income. Similar to an annuity, it offers guaranteed minimum payments and client access to the investments at any time. The funds placed in the variable annuities are invested in a managed portfolio; if investment performance exceeds a contractually guaranteed minimum amount, the payments will also increase in size. Billions of Canadian dollars are invested in variable annuities. Charities can be assigned as a successor annuitant to receive residual income or as a beneficiary to receive a lump sum from the remaining value upon the death of the owner.

Whole life insurance
A whole life policy provides a guaranteed death benefit plus any cash value that has accumulated in the policy over the lifetime of the insured. Some whole life policies pay dividends, which can pay future premiums, received in cash, used as collateral for loans, or used to purchase paid-up additional insurance. There is also an option for an owner to use the accumulated dividends to self-fund the policy, which may result in a lower death benefit – *see reduced paid-up life insurance policy*.

Year renewal term insurance
(*Also known as YRT; increasing term insurance; annual renewal term insurance*). One-year term life insurance policy with premiums based on the owner's age and other risk factors. Premiums increase in every subsequent year that the policy is renewed. Especially attractive to younger people because of its initial low premiums and the payment of a death benefit to named beneficiaries if the policyholder passes away within the year term of the contract, but annual renewal and increasing premiums often lead to policies eventually being terminated.

ABOUT THE AUTHORS

Marlena McCarthy

Marlena McCarthy has worked with charities since 1982 in marketing, communications and fundraising. As Founding Partner and Fundraising and Communications Director of Bequest Insurance (www.bequestinsurance.ca), Marlena works with charities to help create income streams from gifts of life insurance and insurance products by creating simple yet gripping promotional materials. Through her Done Write Communications business (www.donewrite.com), Marlena acts as a fundraising consultant and writer for non-profits, specializing in planned giving promotion, direct mail fundraising, mid-level donor programs, and donor communications materials. In her spare time, she loves singing with her a cappella quartet Spadina Station, and chumming around with her husband, Jack Bergmans.

Jack Bergmans

As a founding partner of Bequest Insurance, Jack is one of Canada's leading experts in integrating insurance into financial, estate and legacy planning. Jack is a Certified Financial Planner and has been in the investment industry since 1996. As a licensed insurance broker, he works with individuals and organizations providing independent financial, investment and retirement advice, and is also an estate planning and legacy giving specialist. Jack has previously worked in various financial planning roles with Manulife Financial, BMO Nesbitt Burns and Altamira Financial Services. Jack can also be found on a golf course, tennis court or bowling alley, and putting his creative culinary talents to good use cooking for his wife Marlena McCarthy and their friends.

www.ingramcontent.com/pod-product-compliance
Lightning Source LLC
Chambersburg PA
CBHW071133280326
41935CB00010B/1202